GLASS HOUSE

PAUL ZEPPELIN

GLASS HOUSE

iUniverse books may be ordered through booksellers or by contacting:

iUniverse
1663 Liberty Drive
Bloomington, IN 47403
www.iuniverse.com
844-349-9409

Because of the dynamic nature of the Internet, any web addresses or links contained in this book may have changed since publication and may no longer be valid. The views expressed in this work are solely those of the author and do not necessarily reflect the views of the publisher, and the publisher hereby disclaims any responsibility for them.

Any people depicted in stock imagery provided by Getty Images are models, and such images are being used for illustrative purposes only. Certain stock imagery © Getty Images.

ISBN: 978-1-6632-6553-1 (sc)
ISBN: 978-1-6632-6554-8 (e)

Library of Congress Control Number: 2024915783

Print information available on the last page.

iUniverse rev. date: 08/01/2024

Contents

Foreword

Paul Zeppelin writes his poetry as a passionate but convincing stream of bright ideas, intense emotions, and laconic clarity without any taboos, whatsoever. He comfortably writes about "Forbidden issues" as religions, sex, politics, and ethics. His verses unearth the deepest layers of our beliefs and doubts, of our dreams and hopes. There is an ancient proverb: "Only the mirrors are sinless."

Paul tried to be a "cold-blooded" mirror reflecting the world we dwell in, but quickly realized that his vibrant curiosity led him into a "no-way-out" labyrinth of, at times, dark conclusions about humans as such.

Being a pragmatic optimist, he often sees a ray of light at the end of his lifelong journey.

Judith Parrish Broadbent
Author of *Golden Days: Stories and Poems of the Central South and Beyond*

A Breezy Shade

Love doesn't conquer hate
As I believed for many years;
Brotherly good and evil wait
To kill or heal our sticky fears.

An eye for an eye,
A life for a life.
No angels in the sky,
Only a falling knife.

I turned two cheeks,
I couldn't fetch the third;
I am surrounded by freaks,
Life is a display of the absurd.

Or rather is a dark charade:
I am broke; I am not choosy,
And I am sitting on the grass
Wrapped in a breezy shade,
I had a smoke and I am woozy,
Time plunges in my hourglass.

I outlived my pension,
Old friends don't ever call;
I don't believe in my ascension,
I do believe in my inevitable fall.

A Haystack

A haystack was our precious bed
Under a quilt of polka-dotted skies,
My tender and caressing hand
Brought ecstasy.
You closed your eyes.

We were so carelessly insane,
Ignoring everlasting serenade
Sung by the wispy strings of rain
For innocence of my virgin maid.

The trees unveiled their faces,
And pawned the gold of leaves,
The early winter's frosty traces
Strolled in a labyrinth of dreams.

A haystack was our precious bed
Under a quilt of polka-dotted skies,
Your tender and caressing hand
Brought peace.
We closed our eyes.

A Swan Before the Slaughter

Under the innocence of light,
She is
A swan before the slaughter.
Wrapped in a gauze of night,
She is
Somebody's loving daughter.

She's dancing naked on the pole,
A gloomy spectacle of badness,
The most heart-searching role,
A tender miracle of sadness.

She is a miracle of broken hearts,
She is a sadness of castrated arts,
She is a miracle of flying dreams,
She is a sadness of dry streams,
She is a miracle of our universe,
She is a sadness of a happy verse.

Life kills, but makes her stronger,
Old Nietzsche was too clever,
To write some other sullen lines.
She couldn't wait much longer,
She undertook a difficult endeavor,
She linked the truths with rhymes.

Whatever someone asks,
She answers with a naked truth,
She throws away her masks,
But wearing only one, her youth.

Adagio G Minor

My dreams decided to return,
And slide by the slopes of hills,
They used to climb the poles
Of arrogant impatience,
Yet never reached their goals
And destinations.

The bridges weren't burned,
Long live, my vile dreams
They have returned
Gift-wrapped in beams
As terrible nightmares
To scorch me in their flares.

All of a sudden, carefully plaited, emotionally charged,
Tranquility of sounds filled my room:
Magnificent Adagio of great Tomaso Albinoni,
Miraculously resurrected by talents of Giazotto
From a few sacred notes left on a tattered paper.
I think he wrote it but took the truth into his final grotto.
Tides of this gentle music lifted all safe-harbored boats
In my forever thirsty soul plague-ridden by eternal youth.

I watch my visions soar:
Old dreams don't entertain me anymore,
But I still hear that Albinoni's masterpiece
Of endless love; of endless peace.

Airborne

When I am dead,
I beg you, never mourn,
Don't sit and cry at my deathbed,
I'll be free, at last; I'll be airborne.

There is a great passion and ferocity
In the way
I go after luscious meals and wines;
There is a deep empathy and curiosity
In the way
I move my wheels between the lines.
Life is a convoluted riddle;
I write and move my threaded needle
Along the olden, rhymed guidelines…

As a young painter
And as an old poet
I've been hailed
And even hated,
But I have never failed
To be a wondering creator.

Andrew Jackson Twenty

Poetic waters are quite choppy,
But I have learned, at any rate:
Bad poets copy,
Good poets imitate,
Great poets steal…

I never knew my birthright fate.

I write, they publish, and I wait
To see a rip-off or a better deal.

But I'm driven by the works of others
Into the gangs of my poetic brothers.

My champagne life of chances
Brings endless sparkly misses;
Good fortune's hugs and kisses
Destroy my personal finances…

At last, the guardrails are in place:
I am in the pleasure-seekers race,
March toward the horn of plenty
Along the Andrew Jackson twenty.

Arbeit Macht Frei

I can't forgive. I hate
The words on hellish gate:
"The labor frees", obey.
"Arbeit macht frei"

Defenseless millions went in,
Only a few came out.
An unforgivable and heinous sin
Against the chosen and devout.

"Arbeit macht frei"
The predators save bullets
And simply gas the prey;
The walking shadows of the Jews.
The so-called Lord has no excuse,
He failed them to the fullest.

We heard their bitter sighs,
We watched their hopeless tears,
We saw a question in their eyes,
Unanswered through the years.

It's written by the ancient scribes,
About diamonds in the rough,
About suffering, yet pious tribes,
Deserving our eternal love.

"I've chosen just a few, don't fight my herd,
Or I will punish you," pronounced the Lord.

Don't worry, please,
"Arbeit macht frei"
"The labor frees".
The Judgement day
Arrived too late
To that satanic gate.

Baited

We were created
Nether for kindness
Nor for compassion:
The hooks of evil
Will be forever baited
By the smart or mindless
As if it is a godsent ration
Of our daily bread.

The devil is alive,
God flew away or dead…
That's life.

Before the Final Countdown

New fashion thrives in Paris-town,
Strange types pace up and down,
It is my generation of "has-beens",
We still wear torn-apart blue jeans.

I spill the wine of autumn gloom,
I pay the fine for honoring a tomb
With a half-erased and wilted sign,
"Here's resting Gertrude Stein";
I curse while drinking on the bench;
The only words I learned in French.

The soulless pitted olives,
Like shingles in the brine,
Remind me of new lowlifes,
Improving their bloodline.

These days, I cross the t's,
The I's won't need the dots;
They go downhill from bliss
As disappointed blood clots.

Tailwinds and obstacles
Don't ever matter,
I pick from paper articles
The former and the latter,
But if I ask for liberty,
Life gives me death
And walks me to infinity
To catch my breath.

I won't be buried in Pere Lachaise,
The famous cemetery of Paris-town,
Where every tombstone is a showcase
Of hopes before the final countdown.

Bowties

This coolest bar
Is not a dicey place;
Even a fallen star
Won't leave a trace.

Good Friday turned into a Holy Easter,
Just like a young man into a mister...
Into a celebration of a resurrection,
A celebration of a yet unknown life,
Into a heartbeat of an unending strife
Between dejection and affection...

I am tightly flanked by soused barflies
And their eye-catching naked shoulders,
Led by a few men wearing their bowties,
Inspiring jealousy of several beholders.

My flirting pushed me to a higher ground:
My heart is drumming melodies of lust;
I am intensely carnal pleasures bound,
Impatient to appreciate them if I must.

Burned

There are as always quite a few
With whom I'd like to sleep,
But very, very few
With whom I'd like to wake,
And wake again in love,
Forever fresh and deep.
To whom I'd wave goodbye,
But miss and long for her
Not knowing why.
With whom I'd love to dream
Or silently enjoy sunrises
Forever old, forever new,
And whisper, "I love you".

Before our castle fell apart,
Why didn't we learn to seal it?
Before you broke my heart,
Why didn't you learn to heal it?
We haven't left a single stone
Unturned,
The remnants left, we earned.
I genuinely loved, but learned
No coming back. The bridge
Was burned.

The past was trained by our tomorrows,
Our love was chained to pains of sorrows.

It is too late to weep and rake the beads.
It is a perfect time to reap the ripened deeds.

Cleaning

I am profoundly engaged
In my quite elongated life;
I am not chained or caged,
I am never ever a dull knife.

Ain't that a shame,
I never met my fame.

The triumph of insanities,
The bonfire of the vanities
Tried to erase my accolades;
I guessed the meaning
Of human history charades.

The critics do the cleaning...

Confusions

During the spin of foolish choices,
Well-known as my careless youth,
I guzzled gin until I heard the voices
From wisdom of the already jailed truth.

These days, I am just circling the drain,
I am not a planet orbiting the sun,
I am not a twisting ring around Saturn;
I simply try to make a single turn
To see perhaps my farewell dawn;
And passionately hope, it's not in vain.

It makes a tone of sense,
I shredded my delusions,
I dumped my adolescence
With all its doubts and confusions.

It is a brand-new strife;
I'm in the pursuit of life.

Debating

The modern fashions
Are for boring people,
Who have no taste
To dress themselves...

Old fashions left a ripple
Under the whitish moon;
Old Vogues are waiting
On the dusty shelves
To be reused quite soon.

The night is thrilling,
I'm able and I'm willing...
My senses are debating
Whether or not to wear
My cleanest dirty shirt...
The oldest man's routine.

Before a probable affair
The reasons never win.

Don't Lose Your Head

Cherchez la femme.
You learn
Intentions of the Lamb;
You earn
Perceptions of the day.
Beware:
Don't travel far away;
She's waiting in your bed.
Don't lose your head.

Remember Salome in dance,
John's head bled on a plate,
She wouldn't take a glance,
She knew the Baptist's fate.

Here's a tiny hair I'd like to split,
Perhaps for someone's benefit:
Don't cast the first and only stone;
Wait for the others to participate
And keep in mind the gaudy fable.
One day, you could be left alone,
Performing on the table
Or bleeding on the plate.

Empty Cart

I've never seen my father,
He's never seen his son…
I buried my dear mother;
Farewell; the thrill is gone.

Our burning hearts
Can't save the world;
The death of earnest arts
Erased our primeval word.

I have been wrong
So, goddamn long;
My world is ruined; fell apart,
No place to hide or flee,
I have to push an empty cart;
It is my temporary glee.

I am King Lear; I lost my throne
Then scrabbled in my pocket;
I pulled a gun; I pulled a phone
Then shut the door and locked it.

I made a sacramental call,
And begged my angel to be fair;
He was attentive; never eager;
I pulled all wishes from my soul,
Then sunk into my chair
And pulled the trigger.

Ethereal

My turbulent relationship
With Mexican Tequila
Has ended in divorce:
I took a hefty farewell sip,
Sunk into my chair pillow,
And wrote another verse.

I walked across the jungle of my melancholic verses,
I was much younger when I picked the wisdom morsels;
My wisdom didn't come with age; old age arrives alone
Into the final page, before the friends begin to mourn...

I hate the endless corridors of powers,
Where poets bang on guarded doors;
And waste their lengthy, and dull hours
Just like the old and unattractive whores.

I cherish my ethereal beliefs,
I treasure precious ancient lines
Repeated by the literary thieves
In spite of the inevitable fines.

I tried to munch on every grain of knowledge,
I studied in the Ivy League renowned college,
But actually I learned on the avenues of life
That a cultured mind is sharper than a knife.

Fountainpen

The cutthroat bloody critics
Had pushed me to the brink.

Even my rhymed four-liners,
Besides my fervent limericks
Were written with my heart,
Not with a fountainpen's ink.

Life is the edge of an abyss
I am alive but feel the heat,
And hear my own heartbeat
While marching toward bliss.

I need todays
Before tomorrows
To heal my yesterdays,
And to erase my sorrows.

Garden

God soulfully cried,
After He heard my stories;
He learned, I feverishly tried
To fight my pains and worries.

He watered from the sky
The garden of my soul,
He wiped a teardrop in my eye,
But cordially allowed me to fall.

His all-forgiving heart
Lent me its darker side:
I learned the ancient art
Of envy, vanity, and pride:
Blue heavens waved goodbye,
White snow chilled my soul,
Red cardinals refused to fly,
Black ravens still pass the ball.

But this is what I always knew:
Some have and eat the cake,
Some value all antique,
Some cherish only new;
It's just a traditional mistake,
We aren't actors on a stage;
Some turn another cheek,
Some write another page…

Golden Dimes

In spite of the darkest-before-dawn skies,
Despite the upbeat future-telling stars,
Regardless of the guessing doctors' lies,
The last war said, "you will remember this,
Nobody can erase your memories
Of bloody wounds and hide your scars."

We who survived explosions
Of the folic-shaped ballistic rackets
Often end up in psychiatric clinics,
Where suffer from the tight embraces
Of the blindly irrational straightjackets,
And making happy our merciless critics.

My style has undergone
My critics' literary slaughter;
My verse has undergone the test of times;
Don't toss your poets out with the water,
Among the wimpy silver quarters
We're the only whole-hearted golden dimes.

Here

We're waiting even when our brain
Is telling us, come over here;
We're in the middle of a yellow lane,
No traffic, no accidents, and no fear.

We have a reason
To be here
As strangers or avengers,
As demons or as angels;
We are forever near;
Without leading light, life is a prison.

Old winter disappears,
Young spring arrives unnoticed,
We are surrounded by many peers,
Who are malignly placing losing bids.

Created by the sun
The rays of fame descend at dawn;
They make me almost blind:
The sky is not unclear. It is my mind.

Hurtle

The bodies are mortal
While the souls are not,
I hear their constant hurtle.

The souls don't take refuge,
They eagerly attain salvation.

It is a daily strife,
My life and destiny
Are totally imperfect;
And yet, I'd never imitate
Somebody else's perfect life.

Compassion and humility,
Love and devotion
Are balanced by
Greed and ego,
Lust and envy.

While I hereby
Create a life of purpose…

I Paid a Girl to Strip

I left the filthy motel rooms
And joined exciting masses
In their intelligent discourse,
Inhaling marihuana fumes,
Sipping from tinkling glasses
Supported by Hors d'oeuvres.

The day of reckoning is here,
Fiction and history will merge,
The truths rest on a higher tier,
The lies will undergo a purge.

Better than fire sale prices
Allow me a luscious dinner.
Anticipation of a midlife crisis
Creates a loser from a winner.

In quest for far-off treasures
Even Columbus sunk a ship.
In quest for carnal pleasures
I paid a gorgeous girl to strip.

It's absolutely different with me:
I pay for sex and say goodbye,
Then live in this perpetual glee
Escorted by the finest lullaby,
"When making love was just
For fun,
Those days have gone..."

Is it a star descending
From the sky?
It is a teardrop sliding
From my eye.

In Pain

Life used to lift me up;
Today, it takes me down,
Today, I drink the bitter cup
And wear the halfwit's crown.

My mind is suffering in pain:
There is no sun,
There is no rain;
There is the silence of a void.

There is my dream destroyed.

Instead

Red berries on a perky holly
Lit by the Christmas beams
That block my daily dreams,
Instead of curing melancholy.

The devil used the power of attorney;
I lost the feeling of accomplishment
After a lonely and traumatic journey
Just like a dull cliff-hanging raptor;
I hope that's not what life has meant,
Instead of a never-ending laughter.

My thirst seems endless,
I drink and snooze a lot
Along the piercing rains
Pleasing the devil's plot
Of a cacophony of rails,
Crafting a noisy madness
Of passing lifelong trains
And their knocking wheels
Bringing some dirty deals
Instead of cozy fairytales.

I learned the misery of being blind:
I couldn't heal my littered mind,
I couldn't see the rays of dawn;
Instead, I saw my friends long gone.

Lethargic

If I don't hear the judge's gavel,
If I don't feel the pulse of life,
If I don't know passion,
If I don't read, if I don't travel,
If I don't have a dream;
It means I lost my strife,
It means I lost my self-esteem,
And it's too late for a confession
Of wasted years for self-denying.

I'm alive but it's a lethargic dying.

Minefields

I want to shred to pieces
Each map of our world;
My poems are the only thread
Connecting blisses and abysses.

I peel as the frustrating husks
My entertaining nights and days,
Besides my vivid dawns and dusks;
They overwhelm my life's walkways.

There are too many don'ts and dos;
I carefully tread these cruel minefields:
But yet, I almost always badly lose,
And rather rarely harvest lavish yields.

The wisdom trees grew up too tall,
I cannot see the writing on the wall.

Peeled

True words remain unwritten,
The world remains lie-smitten.

My eyes are peeled,
A war is over; I'm healed...
I'm a pragmatic pessimist,
i write with anger like a beast.

The mediocre poets copy,
The wingless only imitate,
The great ones simply steal.

The night walks through the street,
My verses choke beneath its feet;
Only the young and still naïve,
Convinced, I am a poet, not a thief.

The words are silent like the mimes;
I stroll and carefully pick them up,
They've been in use so many times;
I tactlessly collect them in my cup.

My arms turn out to be wings,
I climbed against headwinds
I wrote for you, my quiet world,
The words nobody ever heard;

My burdens of the past?
Farewell. I am free, at last.

Neon

I fell in love. She had a friend
Essentially superfluous:
The one who doesn't evocate the happy end,
The one who likes a totally unnecessary fuss,
The one who does bad things without pleasure,
The one who plays the vile cacophonic strings,
The one who amasses our debris as treasure…

I used to study geometric arts:
The Pythagorean hypotenuse,
Connected our two loving hearts,
And shaped a triangle of the affair;
It turned into a coldblooded noose
Above my suicide-ready chair.

I took a look ahead:
The brightest neon letters
Nervously winked their "Welcome",
Inviting us, naïve eternal debtors,
To taste the final piece of daily bread…

I changed my mind; I knew the outcome.

Orders

My eyes are peeled,
I analyze the circle I am in;
Some pull, some push; I yield
With no intensity and fire,
But with a sardonic grin,
They knew; I am ready to retire.

I used to take my marching orders
From greedy, but lifeless hoarders,
Who never knew the value,
But always knew the price.

Only the lord may cast the dice
That certainly will land before you.

I have discovered my own beat:
I watch the shows and the news
From the first row seat.
Looks like a victory; I let them lose.

Paradise Lost

Some play the hearts,
Some make the deals,
Some benefit the arts,
Some turn the wheels.

Some even hear the news
And shrug their shoulders;
While a life-volcano spews
Fiery truck-sized boulders.

I am not preaching to the choir,
No one is taken by surprise:
Their souls lost an essential fire,
They lost the promised paradise.

I am an old death-row lifer,
I've read the books of fate,
I was too slow to decipher
What they say. Is it too late?

I sailed along these years,
And tried to do my very best;
I curbed my fears and tears,
But yet, I flunked the final test:
I didn't toss my pair of dice
And lost the evening paradise.

Paradise lost? Surprise!
Long live a mortal paradise!

Pies

Aggressive realism
Of my linguistics
And passive nihilism
Of my logistics
Don't craft the needed words
To reach the yet unknown worlds...

The fury of a dreamless slumber
Wakes up my memories at night;
A razor-lightning, a mallet-thunder
Pursue my soul; I cannot run or hide.

Today, I understood the game;
I tried but couldn't sleep at all;
My hazy past demands its claim,
But I don't want to pay the toll.

Meanwhile, the frozen rivers
Cannot reflect the skies...
It is so cold even the heaven shivers;
The sky is clear. Where are my pies?

Postulates

I've seen a lot of chips and logs,
I know mediocre and luscious wine,
I never give what's holy to the dogs
Nor cast my pearls in front of swine,
I can no longer turn the other cheek
Even during the Passion Week.

I found plenty, but I lost,
I had a lot, but couldn't save,
For friends, I am a loving host,
My foes I have a closer shave.

I hide no aces in my sleeve,
You owe me; pay the bill.
I can forget, but can't forgive,

God will...

Reason

I lost my future "hand over fist":
I stand on a shaky ground,
But yet, I didn't slash my wrist,
When realized-we all hell bound;

Trust me; I'm not hellhound,
And this is not a happy end:
I lost another bosom friend
To blasphemy and horror,
To cruelty and callous treason,
To degradation of the intellect
That sunk our dire Humanity
Into the warmth of a cozy Hell…

I'm leaving for a reason;
Farewell.

Result

We were in love:
She was a hawk,
I was a dove;
We both were equidistant
From the truth.

She was consistent,
She was a wise adult,
She entertained my youth.

She taught, I learned,
And effortlessly earned
A wonderful result.

I truly learned a lot...
Each i received its dot.

Ripples

I'm throwing money
Out of the window with both hands;
No matter, rainy, dark or sunny,
Jueves or Domingo…
I have no other plans.

The Lord knocks on my heart
As if He nails Jesus to the cross;
To me even a gleam reality is art
Under the secret sacred sauce.

What a surprising
Turn of the events:
The sun's no longer rising,
Only the whitish moon ascends
Above the calmly sinning peoples.

They walk on water; leave no ripples.

Fable

She chirped a pretty fable to my ear,
I tenderly caressed her lovely face,
I drowned in her eyes without fear,
I sensed Chanel, but just a trace...

The full moon floated at the gable
Wrapped in the quilt of cloudy skies;
Two candles cried on our coffee table,
It was the final night for our goodbyes.

If loving her was wrong,
Why didn't she talk to me?
She never let me sing my song,
And yet I thought I dwell in glee.

I swigged my "Maker's Mark"
Then soared into a better place,
Where nights are short and dark,
But long and sunny are the days.

I didn't have to walk too far
To break-in my shiny shoes,
The happy strings of my guitar
Didn't yet learn to play the blues.

I lost the scent of her perfume,
Forgot the color of her eyes,
New daffodils already bloom
Under the springtime melting ice.

Sleeping Car

If we don't know where we're going,
Then any road takes us there,
Where baby-dawns are growing,
Predicting our wonderful affair...

Time rocks our sleeping car
Along the never-ending miles;
Time generously ushered us afar
And let dawns drown in your eyes...

The mirrors of infinity
Reflect the frugal generosity,
Of those who gave away virginity
While entertaining healthy curiosity...

Spring quickly passed away,
I dared to call her in July...
I brought her a bouquet,
I wore my only suit-and-tie...
I simply wanted her to say:
"Your flowers will never die."

Soulless

A chimney-tombstone stands:
It is a skeleton; an empty cage;
It is a heartless, soulless chest,
It is a carcass of a frozen house,
It is a monument of my despair.
I hear profanity-laced rants
Of every high-pitched louse,
The madcaps do their best
With their pretentious rage;
A noise I can no longer bear.

A circus left your town,
You heard the cheers;
I stayed, I am the clown
That wipes your tears…

But then, look in my eyes,
In these two empty wells;
They cannot see the skies
Where our future dwells.

A circus left your tiny town,
I stayed. I am just a clown.

Striptease

The whiny trains of our old railways
Run noisy rains into my foggy days;
I hardly close my eyes, so I won't miss the boons
Of quiet gloomy skies eclipsing enigmatic moons.

I like these lonely nights without friends and foes,
Without wrong or rights, without poetry and prose.
Here is my true identity; I am a man of solitude,
I choose a short serenity over the endless feud.

I know, I have many faults,
But don't accuse me in maturity,
The lemon isn't worth the squeeze;
I fly above the ancient empty vaults,
Above the dungeons of obscurity,
Above the golden autumn trees
And their unavoidable striptease.

I love these lonely starry nights
Without wrongs, without rights…

The Cruelty of Life

I squandered many years,
Under Saint Peter's Dome,
My tired conscience veers
Away from ancient Rome.

The world is not about faith,
It is about artificial power:
We are revolving in a lathe,
And waiting for a happy hour.

I quaff my luscious wine,
I cheat on useless rules;
Our roots are not divine,
We live among the mules.

Looks matter to the mind,
Mean nothing to the blind.

Who are these people?
Who are these strangers?
Only a tiny rolling ripple
Of never-ending dangers.

The cruelty of life,
Is like a rhapsody in gray,
And yet, I learned to thrive
In premonition of another day.

The Graves I Never Dug

I search the rubbles of graves I never dug,
And hide the troubles, I swept under the rug.

My angel never spoke to my direct ancestors,
Those heavy boozers that vanished broke;
Unfortunate investors, accomplished losers.

My tired shadow hides in whispers of the trees
Like bright exotic birds, like first-kissed brides
Performing a striptease for legally blind hordes.

The wingless angel, the prince of fighting,
That vicious stranger removed my pledges,
Destroyed my writing, burned all the pages.

Life doesn't ever end like a nostalgic song,
Like a forgotten verse, or like a useless trend.
I simply said, "So long, farewell my universe."

I wonder if I will be unfit for crazy predecessors,
I bet they fell into the pit for obstinate aggressors.

Tombstone

In French, Je suis un ami d'une maison;
In Spanish, Soy amigo de una casa;
In English, I am a friend of a house.
Each one of us may be a second mouse,
The one who always gets the cheese...

I was forgiven standing on my knees;
They carved my name on a tombstone;
Life after death is just a kiss-or-miss:
The innocently fallen angel
Not any longer is a stranger,
He is my trusted chaperone.

One day we fly above the seven seas,
Another day, we have to visit the abyss.

Trapeze

Our infinity will end,
I'd even say quite soon;
The sun will burn the moon,
The sea will swallow land,
The stars will disappear,
Red wine will morph
Into a yellow beer...

I write about life
Exactly as it is,
I only briefly comment
Then ruthlessly record;
I cut the mother's cord
Flew into a fated bliss,
But failed to descent...

I flex against the breeze
Across the sunny slopes;
I am a fool on a trapeze,
Above my sinking hopes.

Values

A pile of futile values
Wrapped in the faulty rules
Waits on my kitchen table;
I'm too old to use; I'm not able.

I navigate the choppy seas
Of hopes and dreams of plenty,
Surrounded with literary weeds
And nasty views of naked trees
Above my verses no one reads;
My heart is painfully empty…

No man gets less out of a day,
A dubious success some glorify,
My conscious in a grim hallway
Quietly hissed: just say goodbye.

Waltzing

A dark and murky yesterday
Fused with a bright tomorrow,
Delivers birth to a gray today'
My tortured, devastated heart
Wrapped in a sheet of sorrow,
Lies on a butcher's nasty tray
But wants a happy life to start.

I didn't choose to hibernate;
My life is hanging on a hair,
I can't afford to patiently wait
For the avoidable nightmare.

Fresh chill of winter snows,
A loud echo of spring rains
Foretell the summer glows,
Predict the cruel hurricanes.

While I was watching falls
Of waltzing yellow leaves,
These golden bits of a life;
The callous wrecking balls,
No hesitations, fears or ifs,
Have lost this parting strife.

Wink

My life without any reason
Became a silly, dreary nook;
I conned and went to prison
Just to become a real crook.

Without a-nod-and-a-wink
I lost a common sense of joy;
But I can still enjoy a drink
And never be a whipping boy.

My dream-no one can touch,
Entirely belongs to me;
At times, it's not enough
At times, it is too much;
It is my wisdom tree,
It is my still unanswered love.

That throne is unsurmountable
And, though, I'm not a mighty king,
I'm consciously accountable,
I bought a gorgeous wedding ring.

Wreaths

Dunes whisper to the wind,
The ebbs caress the sand
But whip the fishing gear...
A sign "Keep Off" is pinned
Along the trembling pier,
A hopeless, pitiful demand.

The fishermen will fish,
Their wives will wait,
And share a single wish:
"Return, despite your fate."

The boat gone down in a storm;
Only a few nasty seagulls swarm
Above the drowned sailors...
But a so-called Fisherman of Souls
Still hides His faults and failures
On the unwritten pages
Of the Dead Sea scrolls...

Poor wives may hope and wait,
Their dreams will never drown;
They follow the centuries-old trait:
They'll climb that trembling pier
And let their wreaths fall down.

A Melting River

I've heard, winter got lost,
I'm sure, it won't be found,
The lace of window's frost
Melted away spring bound.

March has no time to sway,
April the fool is on the way.

The spring arrived too soon
Upon a slowly melting river
The trees are cold 'n shiver,
Forgotten by the lazy moon.

A sleepless fish
Flirts with my line,
The moon-quiche
Drowns in a brine.

Late night of spring,
The dogs don't bark,
The birds don't sing,
I sip my "Maker's Mark".

A Gypsy Lady

I watch a morbid march
Of self-inflicting doubts,
Under the crispy starch
Of aimless cotton clouds.

Nostalgic dreams at work,
Most problems of today
Morph into the morrows,
We're waiting for a stork,
Good flies above the fray,
Evil remains in burrows.

The great Messiah came,
Then went to join his Dad,
I wonder, whom to blame
A good, an ugly or a bad?
All three stand on my way,
All three brought lovely gifts,
Three wise men of today,
Under the star that drifts.

I'm clever as an owl,
But I'm yet not blind
And see another war.
It's not a proper day
To lose my mind
And throw in a towel,
Then shut the door
And fly above the fray.

The rockets and warplanes
Cast shadows on the slope,
Soaked with the bullet's rains,
And yet, I see a vault of hope.

It is a dialectic flare
Within eternal freeze,
I sense a love affair
Of war and peace.

A Vivid Flowerbed of Endless Love

A vivid flowerbed of endless love,
A mighty magnet of eager souls,
The one I was still dreaming of,
While hiding in the rabbit holes.

I outlived my yearnings' zest,
I blame a headache when I fail,
My inspiration strokes my chest
As if it is a verse carved in Braille.

Behind a mask of hippie-bangles
I hide a shameful dementia galore,
My mind only rejects or tangles,
But can no longer keep the score.

I move ahead by leaps and bounds
Sideways my grossly deviated fate,
Between the hordes of outliers,
And hardly keep my wobbly footing.
While making rather futile rounds,
I realized it's probably too late
To turn the other cheek to liars
Or stop my loyal friends from looting
The tarnished and yet priceless gold
Of gaudy images and joints I rolled,
From verses of my burlesque role,
From hidden treasures of my soul,
Which they don't know, I have sold,
They missed. Gods broke the mold.

Afterlife

I passionately veer
Across my busy life,
But never ever hear
The promises of afterlife:
I watch the warning signs,
At times…

The history doesn't repeat itself;
It only vaguely rhymes;
We pull the older books
From a spider-webbed dusty shelf,
Then read them with learned looks,
At times…

Ancient Myths

I relish my reappearing thoughts
About brightest, enigmatic minds
And fascinating, charming ghosts
Of ancient myths and precious finds.

I wouldn't even try to sugarcoat
The silliness of the Olympic gods;
Instead, I steer away my sailboat
From their vindictive lightning rods.

The sparkling rays of Homer's mind,
The magic music of his luring words,
The piercing vision of this poet-blind
Paved our civilization's endless roads.

They built the solid foundations
For our philosophies and faiths;
For governing of modern nations,
For our democracies' eternal lathes,

I daily read these wisest myths,
Their vailed and multilayered truths;
I often place my unassuming wreaths
On a crumbled tombstone of my youth.

Tealeaves

I read the tealeaves every day,
They say, "You'll finish in a ditch,
Completely blinded by the glow
And glamour of your final pitch
Beyond the blinking Milky Way
Into the world we yet don't know."

It's all descending from the skies:
All those who passionately loved,
Who knew and even lived in glee,
Should never close their eyes;
They have to see each one of us
While poetry still talks and sings,
And we are eager to discuss
The loves of puppets and the kings.

As I comb through the web of art,
I see a diamond in the rough;
It is my bleeding broken heart,
But I don't whine or flaunt and bluff.

No matter what the age,
No one yet really died from love,
It only happens only on the stage.

Bathroom

Under a sweaty bathroom mirror
I found a new a razor on a shelf;
Who am I; a villain or a hero?
I try to calmly analyze myself:

"Forever agitated,
Highly dramatic
And fervently intense,
Respected, loved or hated;
Never dogmatic, yet ecstatic
And wholly in the present tense."

But if I will ever change
And turn into a low hanging fruit;
Please, take me to a firing range
And mercilessly shoot.

Bonjour Sadness

The heat descends like golden locks,
My idle dreams sleep on a lazy tide
That laps against rust-colored rocks
Below a rough hillside
Engraved with evergreen pinewoods,
A garden of my ever-changing moods.

I am curious but quickly bored;
My noon nirvana left a wrong impression
Just like an ancient shiny polished sword
Disguising its pitiless aggression.

Just like a silky lulling spider web,
A calming sticky deadly wrap,
A blanket for a never-ending nap,
A ruthless immortality of total ebb.

Bruised

I put all my chips on losing a number,
My ego and my confidents are bruised,
I am disillusioned, nervous and confused;
I move ahead but hit my future's bumper
My fortune turned to me its back,
Am I a loser, am I a total wreck.

I do my cartwheels in the morning,
I meet my shrink from ten to noon,
And daily hear his nasty warning:
You'll see your angels pretty soon.

Charlatans

Some questions never die,
Some answers never live;
All in the eye of the beholder;
This theory is even older
Then the initial sin of Eve.

Our shadows always follow us,
They know every minus, every plus,
They know every lie and every truth,
They witnessed our troubled youth.

The diamonds of morning dew
Slept under a blanket of the night;
The tree of knowledge slowly grew
For our cunning charlatans delight.

Comprehend

It's Easter Sunday; I'm in church
Trying to find something sacred,
Throwing a hundred on the tray,
Desiring to enhance my search
Beyond our normal daily hatred,
Beyond the tiresome Milky Way
Into the dungeons of the gods,
Into the ordinary fifty-fifty odds.

I simply put my best foot forward
Into the innocence of our youth
To hear again the primal word,
To comprehend the real truth.

David

It was a total watershed in life;
Again, I work from eight to five.
But I am a pragmatic pessimist.

Some strongly argue, but I insist:
The more you sleep,
The less you know;
The more you know,
The less you sleep.

Some may expect a second chance:
Even the first one was hard enough,
A second life is not a second dance,
Is not a better tango with a new love.
They even say,
There's no daylight between the two;
I say, even
If God exists, He wouldn't have a clue.

I carve the mindless manikins
From the leftover slabs of wood.
I'd rather carve another David
From a marble if I could.

Dense Shadows

My world is like a fable, I outlined it on the map,
Then put it on the table and used it as a wrap.
I peeled dense shadows off the fruitless grounds,
And liberated wilted fruits from the ancient bounds.

Through weary blankets
Youthful blades of grass
Pierce nightly darkness,
Refute the futile dogmas,
Tighten the multicolored
Ribbons beautifying gifts;
The gifts of gentle hopes,
The gifts of fearless love,
The gifts of fiery passion
Carrying delicious meals
Of curiosity and intellect,
Integrity and imagination.

Nobody ever understands
Tongue-twisting speakers;
The demagogic squeakers
Pull rabbits from their hats
While our working classes
Enjoy their empty glasses.

Our pedantic world at work
Blows apart a mighty night;
A trembling beam of dawn
Summons a childless stork,
Requests a courteous swan
To sing about blinding light.

A fading light, a final breath,
It is our night, it is his death.

Donkey

According to our woozy priests,
We are created absolutely equal,
Just like the sheep, not beasts...

I'd like to offer you a tiny sequel:

I guard the well-heeled strangers
With smiley sun-splashed faces
Of sinfully angry wingless angels,
That flaunting their four aces...

Meanwhile, I'm a braying donkey,
Both of my long ears are back,
My clay-legs are a little wonky,
I am fatigued; I am a total wreck.

Even my genuine hee-haw
Sounds like a dull handsaw.

Efforts

I walk the corridors of power,
I cross this torturous terrain,
Even the apples grow sour
Under the downhearted rain.

My last chance weakens,
I am a giant with clay legs:
I put my bets on chickens
Against the golden eggs.

My boat is docked,
My life has failed,
My room is locked,
My hopes are jailed.

I calculated all the odds:
And yet my willful blindness
Forgot the arrogance of gods
And used my futile kindness.

I always turn my eyes
Away from the flying dice;
But ask my angel-savior
To spin them in my favor.

I missed a happy hour,
My efforts died in vain.
I am a trembling flower
Under the freezing rain.

Envelope

There is no free lunch,
Just tell me how much.

Life is for some to throw,
Life is for me to keep,
Life is for the sun to glow,
And for the moon to weep.

The old and murky skies
Don't speak on my behalf;
While a damp cloud cries,
I'm alive: still sin and laugh.

A gentle stream of hope
Became a mighty waterfall;
Nevertheless,
The daring fly, the others crawl,
The angels sealed my envelope;
What is my fate? What is inside?

God beams and lets me guess.

Faults

We argue and we fight,
Our love came to an end,
The longest farewell night,
We fell apart, but didn't bend.

Our lives were squares on chessboards,
The dungeons for the queens and kings,
The knights and bishops used the swords,
While we, the players, pulled the strings.

Life is a stage, life is a theatre,
We are performing in a blinding light,
The wins are sweet, defeats are bitter,
Like loud hurricanes after a quiet night.

No one can outwit the Lord,
The faults were never mine alone,
The only argument we can afford,
The guilty shouldn't cast a stone…

Flying Kites

I liked to watch the flying kites...
The painted long-tailed dragons,
Were tender childhood dreams
Giftwrapped in the sunny beams;
They would disappear at nights
Into my parents' station wagons.

The sleepy moon hangs on a gable;
Meanwhile, my lonesomeness and I
Are sitting at the reserved front table,
And watch a stripper drops her dress
Just like a tree that sheds its leaves;
I am a little tipsy and a bit unstable...
Unless, my trusted memory deceives,
At least, I still remember my address.

Funicular

The awfully squeaky funicular of life
Pushes us up and takes us down
To join the lifelong daily strife…
Life is a vicious red nosed clown.

A normal life is like a festive meal,
Served very hot or cold, or warm,
But only behind the seventh seal
Rests our dream: a perfect storm.

I rang an ancient register
To realize the bottom line;
I'm a hired chosen gladiator
To perish for the cloud nine.

A smart palm reader isn't needed;
The future looms before my eyes;
It's optimistic and it's weeded…

The sun will definitely rise!!!

Giftwrapped

I cannot breathe; I need more air,
My life turned upside-down:
The boneyards fly above the trees,
And wouldn't let me rest in peace,
As if I fed myself to a hungry bear.
The fish are floating in the clouds
There is no place to hide,
It is too late to flight…
The wingless angels can no longer fly,
They're giftwrapped in ancient shrouds.

Even the Mother Nature tries to strip;
Nevertheless, our lives don't stop:
While our deaths continue to weep,
We're enjoying Starbucks coffee shop.

Grin

Nobody stops the rite of spring,
Neither a puppet nor the king;
Society is like a basic math:
If we are equal to the same,
We are equal to each other.
There is a bumpy narrow path
From being lame to shiny fame;
But if you don't care, don't bother.

Freedom of minds and choices
Allows us to raise our voices,
And being almost totally congruent
To see who is dumb or who is fluent,
To see a mindless manikin
Behind that frozen grin.

Yet, our mothers told us every day:
The pots don't call the kettles back;
Just figure out your own track
And never ever look away.

Hearse

A drunken driver of a hearse
Still whistles Dixie past the graves;
It is a burial of a yet unwritten verse;
When wisdom sleeps, nobody saves.

They'll offload and burn the rhymes;
A cruel sentence without any crimes.

My gentle soul already learned to fly…
But I'm not prepared to say goodbye.

Hook out of commission

I have no others shoes to drop,
I have no others cheeks to turn,
I wouldn't even dream to stop
To see what I don't care to learn.

I don't tread water anymore,
I am eager and ready to get in;
I'll crawl or walk, I'll jump or run;
I am a true and doubtless believer.
My problem isn't a mortal sin,
My problem isn't the blazing sun,
My problem is a deteriorating liver.

I walk along the church's nave
To see the images of crucifixion;
I do, but probably naively, crave
To separate the truth from fiction.

I begged creators of the bearded god,
The shrewdest people of the Book
To send the secret agents of Massad
And take me off this out of order hook.

I must go

I asked a maven, "Why do I see
In front of me an empty dish?"
"A star has fallen from the sky,
But you forgot to make a wish."

Two candles crying on my table,
Magician-winter hides the leaves,
It is the final chapter of my fable;
"Amazing grace of naked trees."

It is too late to plow,
It is too late to sow,
The end is here and now
Under the endless snow.

Heavens are waiting
Just like a cozy throw;
The lights are fading,
I must go…

I Tried to be a Saint

It was entirely clear:
I tried to be a saint,
I didn't lie or steal,
I didn't fall or faint.

The saints don't ever sleep,
Their tears wash our faith,
They pray for us and weep
Till sins will learn to bathe.

I am a nervous wreck
I am a shuffled deck,
I am back on Earth,
It is my place of birth.

I gathered every bit of power,
The gods allowed me to earn;
It was my sacramental hour,
But yet, I chose the downturn.

It was from the horse's mouth:
Hell is for the moody North,
Bliss is for the happy South;
I really knew what it is worth:
The former was much better,
Nevertheless, I took the latter.

Some say I waste my life
Of which I am an owner;
They want a smoky dive,
I long for a quiet corner.

I followed Jesus for a while,
I even walked an extra mile
Under the yoke of burdens;
Today, I am a mighty truck
That clears religious hurdles
And wishes y'all good luck.

Inherence

My hands are two big birds,
A pair of dearest friends
Who never waste the words
For arguing about current trends.

My losses will evaporate
Into the fog of recent gains;
Remarkably, in any rate,
Red wine is running in my veins.

Even the dead
May come to love again,
To breathe and drink again,
To eat and have the daily bread.

For sins of parents
We, their children have to pay;
It's like a biblical inherence…
We'll never live above the fray.

Justified

The fear of death
Kills our conscience,
The only murder
Which will be justified
In any earthly court:
There is no judge or guide,
Our survival is the last resort;
No one believes in paradise...

When death is the asking price.

Naïve and blameless,
Pure as a baby's breath,
I run from happiness
Into the arms of death...

Knowledge

Unraveled quilts reveal the mystery
Of our convoluted carnal knowledge.

I am not a scholar of ancient history,
And I, perhaps naively, still believe
That nether our Adam nor his Eve
Signed for the ivy-covered college
To get the basics of sex education
Within foreplays and a penetration.

A few virginities were lost in college;
I solely refined my carnal knowledge.

Mass

I talked about half
As much as I had listened,
But failed to make even a dent
In God's ability to laugh.

The doors don't ever kick me in the ass,
I dig through the unknown; I walk ahead,
You'll never see me at the Sunday mass,
I try to earn the promised daily bread...

I'd hate to face the horrors of tomorrow,
I can no longer fight the stupid of today,
I hope AI will let me borrow
The skills of flying far above the fray...

I hold a crescent by the horn,
The sky is awfully dark,
The stars are deadly worn;
I miss the rainbow's cheery ark.

Middleclass

A middleclass mentality
Is a victorious banality
Of stamped minds
Carried In plastic bags
To boneyards of creativity
By horses wearing blinds
Sidelong half-lifted flags
Under the sunless skies.

Nobody mourns or cries.

Mud

I carefully washed somebody's blood
From hands of my aggressive youth,
As if it was a dry uncomfortable mud,
As if it was an old unnecessary truth.

My life is an enormous question,
It is a mystery without any answers:
Compassion is not my profession,
My thoughts are loud and indecent,
My jokes are like malignant cancers,
Only the dogs can catch their scent.

There is no dense and leafy forest,
Only the lonesome naked trees;
My foggy future is malnourished,
The second mouse got the cheese.

Nativity

Our restless spirits of creativity
Shadow established paradigms
Even in a description of nativity
The baby got a bunch of dimes.

God gives us little time
To earn our daily bread;
We learn to earn
'Till we are dead.

Our photos crawl into the frames;
Our grandchildren
Will not remember our names…

It is another paradigm
Nobody gives a dime.

Obituary Was Never Printed

My publisher deadbolts his door,
My foes routinely laugh and mock,
My friends still carelessly ignore,
My daughters try to stop the clock.

My life marched toe-to-toe
With Matthew's daily prayer,
There was a "quid pro quo"
With my Lord's son and heir.

He always welcomed changes,
He didn't let me suffer in todays,
He sent a pair of angels
To walk with mops and buckets
Across my yesterdays.

Life was too brief; I died last night,
There is no grief, there is no light;
My life-train didn't leave the station,
Heaven upholds the same location;
Nobody's fault, no one has failed,
It is my life that silently derailed...

Obituary was never printed
By the newspaper no-one-reads,
My death was never even hinted
In articles of properties proceeds.

Overcoat

I cannot run my train on time;
Years passed. I am not wiser,
And certainly not stronger…
Though, I take a pill from Pfizer,
I drink tequila with salt and lime
And plan to stroll a little longer.

I heard the rattling sabers,
But didn't pay attention;
I didn't leave my real passion,
The radiantly lit green tables.

I raised the rigging of my boat,
I sailed along the river trough;
A bold-faced boyish cloying;
My inborn doubtfulness was off,
I knew where I was going…
I loathe a coffin as my overcoat.

Pegasus

The wheels of life run downhill,
I won't survive. I signed my will.

Gone with the wind; washed with the rain;
I loved and sinned; life is a dead-end lane
Across the land without trees
Toward the bottomless abyss,
Across the fields without grass
Toward the Sundays with no mass,
Across my foes that always lied to me,
Across the truth reflected in their eyes,
Toward the years without glee,
Toward the skies without pies.

I search, I aim, and I am ready,
I don't perform kabuki dances;
Even the chainsaw Freddy
Would offer you more chances.

I am ready to embrace this night,
I am eager to entomb another day;
I disregarded my birthright:
I'd rather be a predator; never a prey.

Across the solemn skies
Where our souls may thrive,
A winged horse Pegasus still flies:
I carve my verse, hence I am alive.

Pious

What had I missed?
Where had I gone so wrong?

The tiny honest candle dies,
The darkness brings the lies,
The idle heavens open wide;
I tried but couldn't run or hide
On urban wastelands heights
From pious devastating lights.

Beware
The wrath of the god-fearing:
They are religious enough
To loathe, but not to love;
They are stubbornly veering
Along their faith and doubts
Wearing my critics' shrouds.

Pretzel

Even a modest talent creates its foes,
A mediocre person creates its friends;
Although, a guy who's hiking on his toes,
Quite often knows how to meet both ends.

Some of those fiery friends
In due course "bought the farms"...
They didn't use the smoke alarms,
And were decisively unfriended,
They reached the bitter ends,
Before their lives have ended.

I twist myself into a pretzel every day,
And try to satisfy my curiosity
That killed our proverbial cat;
It's not my stinginess or generosity
That show me the shortest way
To reach a mediocrity, we all combat.

Even the thinnest European crepes
Or our coins have two sides,
Even the thickest walls or drapes,
Can't keep us from the godsent lights.

Question

I've heard: forgive your foes,
But don't forget their names;
Just hold your nose
When they'll burn in flames.

I dove into my car
And drove to nip some booze
In my beer-pool beloved bar;
It's not a daily demon's walk,
It's my old habit I won't lose,
I am a happy hour wine hawk.

I am ascending
To the angels' status
As a pledged member
Of a sinless apparatus;
My daily swinging
Begged a question:
Would I consider a dissention
Onto the fallen angel's pew?
Of course; I changed my view.

Rephrasing

Whether it's light or dark,
I'm busy with rephrasing
A fragile tiny spark
Into a fire full-blown.

I'm as always gazing
At the unknown:
At people's faces,
At the exquisite laces
Of their vague desires,
Or at the murky secrets
In their gleaming eyes.

Beyond some failures in my past,
Time will erase lies and mirages;
I hope a bit of innocence will last
After time peels the camouflages.

I cherish even my wasted years
On a few wives and futile peers.

Revolving Doors

I early realized I am the best
Amid all fighters in the ring,
I fight to win and then rest
Till a fat lady starts to sing.
Although these days I hear,
"Your soul is yet unsaved,
Before you climb up here,
Your road must be paved."

Another stolen night
From altars of delight,
I desperately veered
From dusk until sunrise,
Meanwhile you desperately feared
That you' will never close your eyes .

It is a bloodless science
Of endless bloody wars:
The sadness of farewells
Brings gloss to our haloes,
Then ignorance of violence
Spins the revolving doors
From courts to prison cells
And back to our sinful laws.

I mix the lion's petrifying roar
With leaves from a naked tree
And clothe that naked emperor
Who lost the Holy Grail of glee.

My mind makes sentences
From tiny bits of precious gold
And sends them to my verses
Obscured by false pretenses.

Schools

There is no place for genius
In our public schools:
Most tests are light as helium,
Teachers are dumb as mules,
A mere Individuality is crushed,
But mediocrity is at premium,
And simple curiosity is trashed.

We are creating human clones
Attached forever to cellphones.

Since God's Been Gone

Since God's been gone,
Our existence after death
Excludes both pro and con:
No bliss, only a final breath.

The demons and the gods,
The blind among the artists,
Even the atheists and Baptists
Are fused by the lightning rods.

I had some wine from a chalice,
I played a requiem on my violin:
My genuine apostasy of malice,
My ode to a sinless Magdalene.

Sincere apologies were begged,
Pity and clemency were earned;
Those bishops were four-legged,
They took her scrolls and burned.

I am watching burning candles
On the dining table;
Their trembling flames
Whisper a captivating fable
About arguments and scandals,
About wars and other games,
The wicked humans like to play;

On Sunday, they deviously pray.

Softly Lit

Under a swirling down gold
Expertly waltzing its title role,
Along a cavalcade of almost naked trees,
I am shivering from cold, but beg my soul:
"Please, do not doze or fade;
I still don't plan to rest in peace."

I let archangels send her
As my uncalled-for treat;
I even promised to surrender
When we'll "accidently" meet.

The leaves continue to fall
Onto a stringy spider's lace;
A shiny mirror in the wall
Reflects her gorgeous face.

Hi, dear, I am back,
The room is softly lit,
My garb flies to the rack,
Her dress slides to her feet.

Excited bride and groom…
The most intriguing scent
Of innocence in bloom…

You know where we went.

Stairway

I knew the factual anatomy of failure,
I knew the misery of fruitless stress;
For years I lived in a dark alley trailer,
But climbed a stairway to success.

My verses are just tearful obituaries
For my forgotten hopes and dreams;
They are subconscious cherries
Over the yogurts and ice-creams...

I am a merciless poet-gladiator,
I fight my never-ending griefs,
But serve like a cunning waiter
The ornamental literary myths.

Sugarcoated

A white-gloved doctor cut the cord,
My mother numbly thanked the Lord;
She knew her son will change the world,
She knew, I will reinvent the primal word.

I know zilch about life and love,
But I caught a pitch from the above
And stole the second base
Right in the middle of a merciless race;
I knew the third is mine,
The game is almost over,
No matter rain or shine…

Anticipations and premonitions lie,
Imaginations and delusions die…
Today,
I kicked the bucket, bought the farm;
A local paper quickly noted;
Some say,
No man, no harm…
Obituary was sugarcoated.

The End of an Endless Sky

I walked my extra mile,
I stood against the Wailing Wall,
Behaving like a mute bystander.
I knew, God leaves us in a while
As if he has decided to surrender
Foreseeing our endless downfall.

I tightly closed my eyes,
He didn't touch my face,
I saw a magic of his rise,
But didn't seek his grace.

I wished to see the road ahead,
The persevering good and bad,
I wanted to have wings and fly
Into the end of an endless sky.

I trust, the winds will blow,
I trust, the trees will sway,
The river-time will flow,
And wash my sins away.

Farewell. My universe capsized:
Gods judge; the mortals save.
I reached the end and realized,
We'll be equal only in the grave.

Indian Summer

The rite of Indian late summer
Pours rains as a crafty plumber,
Ripens the tiny green tomatoes,
And lovely girls desire to date us.

October has arrived,
September took a ride,
The muddy gush of rains
Swirls into the noisy drains.

From nowhere in my sight,
The sudden angry storms
Swing trees from side to side,
And toss their leafy uniforms.

Our anguish hits the bottom,
Our voices' loud echoes rise,
And even the Holy Phantom
Inches us closer to paradise.

The winds of autumn blow
Great colors in their flights,
The striking rainbows flow
Across the fields of lights.

The naked branches reach the sky
And scratch it with their spiky nails,
The cotton pillows of the clouds fly
Like boats under the happy sails.

Thromboses

I am familiar with only two
Manifestations of reality:
It is our thirst and pain…
Forget our faith and love
As a rundown triviality.

Take care of thromboses
In every artery and vein;
It wouldn't make us stronger,
But we may live much longer.

Twister

Ash Wednesday with its lent
Morphs into Fat Tuesday,
And Mardi Gras;
A happy, wonderful event
Approximately in forty days…
Any religion has its silly ways
To chock us with its paw.

I used to follow all those rules
Before and after Easter,
Until the hurricane of truth
Shattered illusions of my youth.

Long live the liberating twister!

Void

Knowing full well that you are mortal,
Indulge yourself with luscious wines,
Delicious meals and loyal friends,
Then visit every corner of this world
And you may learn the primal word...

And only then you'll die,
And only then your soul will soar,
And only then your soul may need to fly.

It is a void; there's nothing anymore.

Tossed

My Lord,
We don't forgive all those
Who sinned against us,
Your kingdom will not come;
Here is my word:
Only the fallen angel knows
Why he was tossed
Under the bus;
He was exuberantly dumb
And marched to the beat
Of his own drum,
At any cost.

Warped Mirrors

I never knew a nickname of my angel,
I simply tried to recognize his deeds:
Two wings, nevertheless, a stranger
That sowed his good-and-evil seeds.

I lived like a forever hungry shark,
I wrote my lines and hardly ever slept:
I was the only poet on the Noah's ark;
The rest enjoyed my rhymes and wept.

At times, I tread the murky waters
Among the idle bottom feeders,
Often ignored by my greedy readers
In their pursuit of dimes and quarters.

My love remains a hundred kisses deep,
My life streams like a scrumptious wine,
But I am ready for my final leap,
I am ready for my parting breath.
I wish no one will whine,
I wish no one will weep.

Even the duly noted lives of heroes
Will disappear without a trace…
Only my death will leave her ugly face
In dusty, warped, and cunning mirrors.

Wonderland

Cliquish bohemian hinterland,
Opaque and deceptive camouflage,
Kept our secrets tightly canned,
Amid unknown charms of that mirage.

It was a touch of malice,
A straw that killed a camel at the end:
I bought for her red shoes of Alice-
She marched barefoot to wonderland.

She is both Virginia Wolf and Vanessa Bell;
Those rogue and rather enigmatic sisters;
I'd rather drink my water from a rotten well,
Then listen to her hazy convoluted whispers.

Life slipped into a war
Through days and nights,
Through dawns and dusks…
Meanwhile, I keep the score,
And swing from wrongs to rights
Like minds and souls that lost their husks.

A Rearview Mirror

A rearview mirror flaunts
The warmth of yesteryears;
I never miss those days
Of disregarded warnings
About my agonizing pains
Of waking in the mornings.
Unwillingly, I moved ahead:
My verses fell on idle ears,
I praised the brave, but dead.

Jack London or Bret Harte,
I lost and missed them all.
I lost sunrises in my heart,
And stood against the wall
Of troubles and despair;
I climbed; some didn't dare.

I pledged to write the truth
About conflicts of the past,
Not a conniving crafty fiction.
I'll never sugarcoat my youth,
I'll blow off a heavy overcast
Of my inferiority addiction.

My yesterdays don't sing,
My red sunsets don't last,
Life morphed into a boxing ring,
And let me struggle in the past.
I promised to revisit that abyss
To learn the truth from ganders
And totally emancipated geese.

A Saint Must Have A Past

A saint must have a past,
A sinner needs tomorrows,
A soul is a broken plaster cast,
A mausoleum for my sorrows.

I hear the midnight tunes
Of lonesome nightingales,
While quiet silver moons
Guard secrets of my tales.

The memories are often fruitless,
They bring the scars of our flares,
They never bring back goodness
And joy of our passionate affairs.

My scarred and wrinkled face
Etched on a coffin of my years,
I miss the one I would embrace,
She was a witness of my fears.

She left, the skies had flipped,
She left, bliss fell in the abyss,
The angry branches whipped
The bodies of uprooted trees.

My mind is a quaint enclave,
It is a boneyard of my whims,
But I'm still alive and crave
The advent of my dreams.

Absurd

It is the play of the absurd:
I turned two cheeks,
But couldn't fetch a third
For creeps and freaks.

An open-minded metropolis
Of my decaffeinated brains
Prefers the uncontrollable police,
And horses that don't know reins.

Life is a fraught experience for me;
I am just a novice, a mere beginner;
I try to balance to be with not to be:
Am I a dreary saint or a witty sinner?

My soul will never levitate,
It is too heavy with my sins:
I won the losses,
I lost the wins
Amid the boneyard crosses.

In front of me an empty plate.

Adieu

I eat or sleep all day,
I play and drink all night;
I am omnivorous-not vegan,
Soundly vigorous-not deaden.

Two dots on every dice
Remind me of snake eyes...
A face of a never-ending strife
Of our fiery sun vs. eternal ice.

I play blackjack with life:
Two aces never kill,
Only the sevens do...
I often add sixteen to five,
I win and have my thrill,
Then grab my chips. Adieu...

My thirteen bullet gun
Forever cocked and ready;
Although, my luck is on the run,
My eyes and arms are steady.

Aged

We loved and we were one,
We even cast a single shadow
From early evening to a dawn
No matter heat or rain, or snow...

Her brown eyes
Brought joy into my soul;
She always wore a happy mask,
She always played a leading role.

Regrettably, I aged, took ill,
My fears turned into hatred;
A constant misery; no thrill
In everything so dear and sacred.

These days, just mark my word:
Our poetic languages' pathology,
Excuse a pun, is not a dying art;
In our exuberantly modern world
Only the Greek mythology
Consumes my mind and heart.

I hear those ancient voices
Of honest friends and foes,
Or cunning self-admiring heroes
Reflected in the crooked mirrors.

Ambition

A pair of steadfast guards,
Peter and Paul should wait:
I whistled past graveyards
In front of their elusive gate.

The clouds took my feelings to the gods;
I hung on ropes like boxers in the ring,
And asked myself, "What are the odds
For me to live and see the rite of spring?"

I craved to see my fragile paradise,
I craved to justify my premonition,
I craved to see with my own eyes
The promised bliss…
Or yet another egotistical ambition.

Horses got out of the stables,
The fish jumped out of the water
The sun descended to the gables,
My soul escaped the slaughter…

I asked, "Is this the end of our world?"
The saints and angels didn't say a word.

Ancient Psalm

Is life a journey to success?
We never know; our angels guess.
We need a social lubrication
To coexist without being friends:
Even for our wealthy nation,
At times, It helps to meet the ends.

A soothing therapeutic balm
Of skillfully veiled crudeness
Described in the ancient psalm
As common greed of lewdness.

With our black-eyed minds,
With vague and misty wills,
Like horses with the blinds,
We rush past the hazy hills
As greedy brutal go-getters
To catch our hiding debtors.

We often monetize our souls;
It's a coldblooded business;
A caterpillar-time still crawls;
We beg for God's forgiveness.

Anesthetic

My heavy drinking is anesthetics
That let me write and tolerate
The chronic pains of my poor life;
In spite of my refined aesthetics,
Welfare is a constant bloody strife.

Life stored a lot of verses in my mind,
I wrote some new; the oldies rested;
Meanwhile, I wastefully wined and dined
In Paris' bistros where every poet nested.

The swirling, bubbling streams
Of my well-rhymed four-liners
Dug into my hopes and dreams
Like the most skillful coalminers.

I laughed and joked when I was young;
These days, I lost those naughty skills;
Life bared its poisoned riven tongue…
I can no longer drink and pay the bills.

My life became a stinging nettle
And I won't lay my arms and leave;
Don't laugh; I bought the biggest kettle
To boil every problem and let go grief.

Arthur Rimbaud

The sun was trapped
In branches of the tree
Guarding infinity of glee
On my front yard;
Meanwhile, I slept…

The night is cold; I shiver;
The winds were kissing leafs
As if they dropped their griefs
Onto the long black river
And murmured their romance
Into the evening breeze.

"Sur le long fleuve noir
A la brise du soir"
As Arthur Rimbaud wrote…

It was a passing note…
I woke; I didn't want to freeze.

Artichoke

Nestled in a heart of artichoke,
I am the horrid Kafka's roach…
It is a metaphysical approach
For all of us who live to croak…

Who have a totally lackluster life,
Who daily work from eight to five;
Just like a hungry Gregor Samsa,
Just like my badly written stanza,
From a defeatist lack of will to live,
Or from the lack of aces in a sleeve.

A metamorphosis or transfiguration
Are clones of mental masturbation.

Assassins

My saw these movies' wrinkled face
Reflects the endless joy of victories
Against the constant trivial pursuits;
Meanwhile, I wolfed quite a few years,
Then battled tooth and nail my losses,
And plucked the most forbidden fruits,
And laughed into my ceaseless tears…

Our fragile peace deserves a quiet harbor
Above the battlefields and morning dew;
I am sure; we have to work much harder
And build safe castles in the endless blue.

Back then, I met some baby-faced assassins,
They never heard or cared about seven sins;
The calmly pulled the triggers; never aimed;
They've grown up but still are not ashamed
That our life for them was just a barrel
For shooting hapless fish;
I wouldn't sing for them a Christmas carol,
The hell's inferno is my wholehearted wish.

I didn't have to jump through hoops
To prove that I'm a deserving chap;
Nobody hears my wows and oops;
They judge my verses by the wrap.

Bacchus

Forgiven memories of our souls
Fly high above the lavish fields;
Another brassy autumn strolls
Across the rows of juicy yields.

Heavily hanging on a sturdy vine,
The grapes are velvety and dark.
I am singing as a happy lark,
I am dancing on cloud nine!

I burned a bridge of difference
Between two wines;
I swigged them both…
I'm a student of the Renaissance:
I simply read between two lines;
The first was of a second growth.

There's nothing further to discuss:
As Bacchus said: In Vino Veritas!

Barflies

L'amour est mort.

Depression lingers
During our god-nourished happy hours
Among barflies so rarely taking showers,
I see three angels with trembling fingers
Caressing wounded hopes and dreams,
Holding the mirrors to their ashen faces
Flaunting the mesh of wrinkled streams,
They are those ancient neglected traces
Of always convoluted walks of our lives
And doubts left by never-ending strives.

Beer truck

I used to sail from dusk to dawn;
For a strong family it is too long;
My wife arranged to see someone,
And learned to sing the oldest song.

Another careless night
Turned off a blinking star
And sunk into a hazy sadness;
I had to drag my yoke of badness,
I had to lull my life, but went to fight
My friends-barflies into the nearest bar.

Blinded

At times, I make a conscious choice:
I really am myself with the defeated,
But still retaining their own voice
In spite of being poorly treated...

I am not a stubborn tower of strength,
I hardly march on wobbly feet of clay,
I try to keep the demons at full length,
Although, at night, all cats look gray.

What had I missed?
Where had I gone?
I haven't been "abyssed" or "blissed";
I am just blinded by the burning sun.

Boring

A horny gray-haired evening
Is flirting with the lonely moon,
And keeps her foggy dreaming
Away from the good old prune.

I didn't have a wink of sleep,
I'm not yet ready for a weep,
I'm not ready for a dreary bliss,
I'm not ready for its final kiss.

Besides some failures in my past,
I'll leave delusions and mirages;
I hope some innocence will last,
I crave to drop old camouflages.

I left a few totally wasted years
To meet some two-faced peers.

Brazen Horse

I used to stroll along deep wells of endless joy,
I heard the Sunday bells, amazed as a little boy;
My soul embraced the gospel singers;
My jolly youth has been erased. Life lingers...

I've grown constantly corrected; it was a punishable trade;
Even self-righteous saints who died but later resurrected,
Are winged these days, but unrecognizably decayed.
Even in glee I get to ride a brazen horse of life;
I want to see a better side of our futile strife.
And write my verses for the mindless corpses.

Inevitability of death has petrified my youth;
I couldn't catch my breath but I revealed truth:
There is no paradise;
Poor Judas landed on the ice,
Eleven went to the abyss,
Only their boss arrived to bliss.

I left the truth for the minds left far behind:
Evil and good are always neatly intertwined.

Broom

The nuisance if my fight sets me on fire,
My lines are crude that once were tender,
I write as if I walk in circus on the wire;
My critics bark; I write and won't surrender.

I write about malachite of grass,
About diamonds of morning dew,
About autumn's gold and brass,
About endless sky that is still bleu…

The outstanding arts
Each time, a fantasy:
The only worthy poesy
That enters our hearts.

Today, for my own sake,
I threw away the gloom;
I eat and have my cake…

I am not yet flying on a broom.

But at the End

We split some hairs and drown in sophism,
Under the blankets of a pessimistic nihilism.

I hold the enigmatic gem with secrets of the word.
I am at the mighty helm, and flaunt the real world:
Solemnity of laughter, sobriety of quiet cries,
And in the mornings after, the frailty of lives.

Two lovers at the window; two shadows on the floor,
They aimed quite high into the brightest glow;
In vain, they tried to fly, but drowned in the salty flow.

These loves don't cry, they break our hearts,
Their wings don't fly, they only send regards.

I bravely run and zig, I humbly walk and zag
Under a clumsy wig, over the shattered lives,
With a hand-written tag glued to the other lies.

I met my oldest friend; supposed to be a happy day;
We swam in wine; but at the end, all cats look gray.

Long live
Our rhythms of our lives, our self-imposed routines,
Our teardrops in luscious wines of our forgiven sins!

Carriage

Our efforts in the pursuit of glee
Deserve attention of philosophers;
Besides our genes and pedigree,
They Readily Dissect Our Love Offers.

She fell in love with me,
She has become my muse,
We touched the fragile glee,
Walking along the pews.

Life ends in death
Love is a life that also dies,
Only antipathy survives,
Nobody heard its final breath.

It happens to the best of us:
Our love boat untimely sunk
In the quagmire of marriage;
Love cast us under the bus,
And left in a cut-rate carriage.

We still divide our useless junk.

Rhetoric

Despite some notable flashes of success,
I often slide into the pit of useless rhetoric;
I try to show off my courage under stress
In verses it seems euphoric and retro-chic.

The rules created by our high establishment
Allow many crimes exist without punishment
Or cruelest punishments without any crimes-
Melodramatic jurors turn ethics on the dimes.

No guilt,
No sorrows,
No devotions;
We built
Snug burrows;
No emotions.

Cicero

I am steering clear of folly,
Draped in a mild melancholy;
I see a lot of what's,
But not enough of how's;
My curiosity gets scars and cuts
While I am continuing to browse.

I went through a religious sieve
And praise the joy of consolations;
A man must know how to believe
In sacred odds of transfigurations.

Today, I am a speechless Cicero,
I am one of those silent geishas:
I watched the stages of this life
From each and every row
And saw nothing but a bloody strife.

If this is what our Lord created,
We have to ask Him to update it.

Cloudless

I learned where my emotions dwell;
It's in a heart; a bit below my mind;
Subconscious is my wisdom's well,
It's deep and quite obscure inside.

I am correct only two times a day,
Just like the old grandfather clock;
For some it is a quiet time to pray,
For me, it is a monotonous tic-tok…

I waste no time for prayers,
I'd rather watch the soccer players;
I also waste no time for wrath,
I'd rather give my soul a bath.

Only idealistic grooms and brides
Believe in the cloudless tomorrows;
They trust know-it-all angelic guides;
I trust no one will ever loll my sorrows.

Clubbing

I used to prelim my night-clubbing
With a few cans of Guinness beer
To lull my conscience scrubbing,
And drop my law obeying fear...

The beat of my subwoofers thumping
Reminded of the hypertonic hearts
Continually and strongly pumping
New blood into the modern arts.

Crowded

First item every morning,
Last thing before I fall asleep,
I see my dusty copy of a sculpture:
A Mother in her mourning,
Who still continues to weep
Over her Son's divine departure.

This planet is too crowded for us:
Some will ascend to bliss,
Some will be tossed under a bus,
Majority will slide to the abyss.

No one walks on the water;
I'd rather flip a quarter,
And call the tails...
I hardly ever wonder
Whether my fortune
Thrives or fails.

Denials

Life rocks my sleeping car
Along the never-ending miles;
It generously ushers me from far
Into the world of fictions and denials.

The shadows of society
Obscure my solitary strolls
Along the streets of notoriety
Without wishes, aims or goals;
Rejecting never needed help
From kindly passing strangers,
Ignoring constant squeaky yelp
Of angry critics and wingless angels.

All-of-a-sudden, it all ended:
It was a true epiphany,
No doubts, tears and fears;
The tunes of earthly symphony
Had reached my idle ears
And good and evil blended.

Dime

A broken heart cannot be mended with a bandage,
Forgive my rather uninspired use of our language,
But there is no poetry in a decaffeinated silence,
But there are no poet free walkways in science,

My four-lined limericks and vivid verses
Are not the four apocalyptic horses;
They're big monies in the wisdom purses.

We drown in the downpours of mediocrity,
Yet hardly ever tap onto the treasure trough
With the unsurpassed triumphs of antiquity;
A visit to the Sistine chapel is not enough.

Ten even rusty pennies make a dime,
The cornerstone of our greedy paradigm;
A naughty incarnation of all whatever is;
A calculating ruler of bliss and the abyss.

Disappearance

Death
Is a total disappearance
Of lies and innocence,
Of bravery and fears...

But if you ever see my soul,
Take a deep breath;
It means my pure existence
Has never used a birth control.

Dolorosa

The cross was growing
From His bed,
From a pure innocence
Of His first breath,
Foreseeing more
Than thirty years ahead,
The day of Via Dolorosa
And His appalling death.

I don't forget the dead;
Only still living is forgotten;
I do receive my daily bread,
Although, my pledges
Are forever dead or rotten.

Downfall

Our fragile world is sinking,
While we are captains of it all;
The stars are arrogantly blinking
In premonition of our downfall...

As trumpets of aggression,
As crying violins of bliss
Betrayal, love and passion
Brought our farewell kiss.

A mirror on the wall of life
Reflects out wretched years;
At times, a vicious strife
Within our laughs and tears.

In search of the beginning,
We march toward the end;
Deaths slide into our being;
Only the lucky ones ascend.

After extensive sugarcoating,
Only the worthless enter bliss;
The garbage always floating
The worthy enter the abyss.

Drifter

Somebody killed my heart,
Life sang "Amazing Grace";
I miss a well forgotten art,
The warmth of an embrace.

I trudge across each state
From Florida to Maine,
Devoted to a drifter's fate,
No matter shine or rain.

I meander with these guys,
We're trading boring jokes,
Eat burgers and french-fries,
Just happy clams. No yokes.

My exodus wasn't liberation,
I clamed no places as my own;
My train already left the station;
I'm pleasing my curiosity alone.

These days, I stomp the west
From San-Diego to Seattle,
Enjoying weed and all the rest;
I'm looking for a place to settle.

I heard some other drums,
I rambled to the other beats
I marched across the slums;
A single victory in my defeats,

My past went into the blur,
My future wouldn't show up;
And as The Son so fearful of death,
I sobbed; The Father heard my slur:
"Don't let me drink that cup,
Don't take my final breath!"

Eclipsed

Springtime arrived again,
A godsent timeless truth
Destined to bear my pain,
A bitter echo of sweet youth.

I am playing solo on a violin,
I am playing solos all my life:
Just like a childlike harlequin;
Persistent as a falling knife.

My tunes are raw and coarse;
Impulsive as a loaded gun;
I gallop like a nervous horse
Under the wholly eclipsed sun.

I know, love will find me,
Bright as a flower in the grass;
The greatest wine of glee,
Delightful in every glass.

I am a bee that lost his hive,
I miss the tunes, I am alone;
My solo is a lifelong strife:
The play must go on.

Elitist

I carved this story from my tomb,
St. Mathew is my Nom de Plume.

I used to be a staunch elitist,
But never ever was a snob;
I was indeed not a defeatist,
I never stopped, I did the job.

My critics labeled me a crusher,
They craved to engineer my soul,
They bribed my idle angel-usher
And smashed the guarding wall.

The Last, the parting Supper
Was served in the upper room;
It wasn't only gloom and doom:
The twelve received His body,
The twelve received His blood;
Or better yet, they drank His wine
And thoroughly enjoyed His bread;
But at the end, He desolately said
That one of them will end His line,
And that is His Father's final goal.

King Sol will build the Wailing Wall.

Endorphin

The "feel good" chemicals,
The serotonin or endorphin
Are old, worn-out testicles;
That won't allow us to sin.

No one is right, no one is wrong,
Though, love gets more uncertain;
Life is forever an unknown song,
I hope to sing it till the final curtain.

Enough Rope

A bird may sing her song,
Then dive into the night...
I carve my verses all nightlong
Until I sense the warmth of light.

I have just enough rope
To hang myself,
While my uplifting books
Are dying on a dusty shelf...

Excitement left my daily maze,
I am writing tragedies these days
About futile, self-effacing jesters;
A sad satire about my ancestors.

I never sought a path from joys to woes,
I daily fought my critics-my vicious foes.

I truly hate to be intimidated
Or undeservedly harassed...
Regrettably, my books remain ill-fated,
I am a starving poet but not half-assed.

Erratic Sky

Pass by, don't envy, and forgive my glee,
I know wounds and pain; I know anguish;
I have a troubled life, but never languish;
I'm still fighting; I'll never even try to flee.

Under the blue, unstable and erratic sky
I live without any gods,
Without any angels, without any saints;
I hide from the merciless lightning rods
Between the arches of the seven paints.

I keep my head and shoulders
Above the never-ending fray,
And yet, I push the literary boulders
In spite of shaky arms and feet of clay.

Dusk always morphs into the night;
No colors, all in black-and-white…
It is my promised paradise. I write.

Escape

The truth stands right in front of us
Or lies on the bottom of some well;
We live as if we try to catch the bus
From which we miserably fell.

Selections made by Paul and Peter
Created rather sour and bitter grapes
Of our future, gloomy and uncertain…

Therefore, our jolly optimism escapes
From our life's long-winded theatre,
And pulls the last, concluding curtain.

Filigree

My sybaritic life is obvious to all,
In the pursuit of self-indulgence
A pleasure is my only chosen aim;
I traveled to the Western Wall,
God heard my southern drawl
And let me live my life and claim
The joy of epicurean abundance.

Even the saints pledged to return
And spend more time with me;
They wanted me to learn
Not only rough 'n tough but filigree.

Before I learned to write,
I learned to live,
I learned to love,
I learned to fight;
When that was not enough,
I learned to laugh,
And only then I learned to cry
Under the blanket of the night.

Years passed; today, it is too late
To resurrect my dreams and hopes,
I hung them on the heaven's gate;
The guiltless fallen angel asked me
To bring not only the lacy filigree
But tough 'n rough, long-lasting ropes.

Friday Night

I can't acquire my glee again,
Limelight is a great pretender.
Small talks with a bartender
And a sweet cocktail waitress,
Both frivolous and brainless.

Some young and pretty,
Some old and wrinkled,
Well-mannered hookers
Flaunt their merchandise
Wrapped in deodorants.

The ice cubes' crackling
Dilute our precious drinks.
I take my "Maker's Mark"
As always neat
In a warm cognac snifter;
I haven't lost the beat.

Sharp loud voices
From the billiard tables
Attract red-blooded men
To try their lucks;
I played a game of snookers
And "pooled" some extra bucks,
While a few eager hookers,
Lined up like a bunch of ducks.

A slowly crawling Friday night
For those who hope to drown
Their aloneness in the crowd
Of a gloomy happy hour delight.

I have no skin in daily games,
I am thinking like a lonely dove
I willfully reject all fragile aims,
But one: a never-ending of love.

Frog

I'm Paul.
When Peter rested,
As our Lord requested,
I held the keys from heaven,
But hardly used them for a while:
Majority of us were not acquitted
During the final trial.

They were decisively defeated.

The more I know people,
The more I like my dog…
Just try to kiss a prince,
He'll morph into a frog.

Genesis

Paleontologists discovered
The region we all derived from:
A Sub-Sahara sunset-colored
And spicy as a Jamaican rum.

We lost our paradise,
But can't forget the Eden;
Our never thrown dice
Remaining safely hidden.

We strolled through centuries
Forever exuberantly traveled;
Though pits and penitentiaries
Of murky mysteries unraveled;
Across the scheming rhetoric
Of taken from a thin air record
Of life opaque and prehistoric,
Still hanging on a mother cord.

To our surprise
Hopes dissipated;
We couldn't recognize
The lives of our primal parents
Often too shamelessly X-rated
Under the heaven's sunlit dome:
No Adams and no Eves;
Only the Tree of Wisdom
And its fallen golden leaves.

George

I watch the rearview mirror,
The memories don't ever die,
The actors look much clearer
Under the downhearted sky.

Nobody guards the gates,
The scared King trembles,
The princess tearfully waits,
The dragon boldly gambles.

The seven-headed beast,
Wrapped in a fiery steam,
Self-righteously unbowed,
Anticipating a luscious feast;
A posterchild of self-esteem
Without indication of a doubt.

But at the end of this annoying story
St. George set free the gorgeous girl,
And lives in the eternal fame and glory.

Gloves

We both are watching our street
Thru a widely parted curtain,
Our kids are asking trick-or-treat,
But I'm terrified; you're uncertain:
If you will ever change your mind
About leaving me behind,
We will remain two loving doves,
Who never walk or fly apart;
Here is my life; here is my heart,
They missed your velvet gloves.

Under her shawl of doubts,
Under my jacket of despair,
The same cruel evil flouts,
We should no longer bear.

Goodbye, Be Well

The foreign flags
Flap in the breeze,
The tourists drag their bags
And fight the evening freeze.

I walk along the river's flow,
I stroll across the ancient park,
I'm from Nashville to say hello,
But Moscow sleeps, it's dark.

A country scraps, it's only fair,
The city didn't lose its flair;
The old regime is banished,
The pedestals without heroes,
Some villains fell and vanished
Into the fog of smoky mirrors.

The anxious city of my birth,
The honey-river of the past,
The sweetest place on earth,
Nostalgic youth arrived, at last.

Old Russia hides behind the walls,
New USA with lures of freedom;
I shared my life between two souls-
I lost my folly, gained my wisdom.

I waved my hand,
Goodbye, be well-
I crossed the land to say farewell
To heavy burdens of the past;
I wave my hand, goodbye, be well,
I am forever free, at last.

Hamlet

Read a good book,
Drop your illusions,
Learn basic history,
Get off the hook,
Unveil the mystery,
Dismiss confusions.

As an alleged pathfinder
He wandered in his glee,
And mumbled as a whiner:
"To be or not to be?"

Surrounded with blowhards,
He let them have his lunch
Those miserable bastards
Wolfed without any crunch.

A skimpy loner Hamlet,
A nerd beyond repair,
I wish he'd not lament,
I wish he'd have a love affair;
There were some chicks to furl,
A prince could always get a girl.

I wish he would have a son.
I could enjoy a longer story,
But now he is dead and gone,
Shakespeare got all the glory.

Harlequin

Life fell into my hands
As a Black Friday sale
Of everlasting heavens;
The gloomy future ends:
Even a single nightingale
Fend off the feisty ravens.

Lights drowned in the sea,
The end of a fiery sunset;
Life brings the days of glee,
But cannot raise the dead.

Hogwash

She was a pocket woman
As the French doyens say:
"Une femme de poche".
I loved her anyway…
It didn't break the dam
In spite of their hogwash.

I stirred my life,
I didn't rake loose ends
And lost my wife…

I touched the stars
But burned my hands;
I healed the scars,
The wounds remain…
Friends think I am insane.

Holocaust

My gypsy-future didn't hold my hand,
And didn't follow every scar or line,
But just as a canary in the mine,
Predicted every vital trend…

I picked a diamond of frozen water
Reflecting in its every facet
The ancient teeter-totter
Of our unpaid horrific debt
To those who outlived that slaughter,
And simply asked us never to forget.

Hymns

Remains of our crimes,
Those shattered molds
Of our astounding nights
Play jingles of these times;
We wait 'till darkness folds
And sing the hymns to lights,
Descending on modern ears,
A fertile place for many years.

It is a journey,
Not a destination,
A silent tourney
Through our elation.
A day of madness
Becomes a toy,
A drop of sadness
Gives birth to our joy.

I am a fearless guard
Of intellectuals and coy,
I didn't sell my broken heart
To idle angels' sybaritic ploy.

The honors are still falling
On my retiring shoulders,
My verses are still rolling
Like Sisyphean boulders.

I run from those who reign,
From our heroes canonized,
Respected-hardly loved;
But strangely, once again
I want to be baptized
By someone velvet-gloved.

I Led Her to Sunset

I acted as a puppeteer
Over a cute marionette;
I led her to a red sunset,
But found just a tiny nook;
She gave me all. I took.

It was our first sunset,
It was our happy night,
She thought it was a debt,
I thought it's my birthright.

She was a bird in hand…
I whispered common lies,
She rose above the land,
Skies mirrored in her eyes.

A nervous coexistence
Of our independent plays,
Of horrid days and nights,
Hands us some distance,
While Nike humbly prays
Observing our cruel fights.

She wore a shawl of irony,
I wore a jacket of despair;
We could no longer bear
A day of our own tyranny…

I Painted a Self-Portrait

I painted a self-portrait:
My vanity in a rectangle,
My features kindly sorted,
My wrinkles were untangled;
It was a well lacquered truth
About my evaporating youth.

Life's crawling forward only,
I can't return to yesterdays,
I am bored and I am lonely,
There's nobody to embrace.

I am sick of metronomic hearts,
Of their anemic lifeless charts;
I wish to see a bright someone,
To meet together a new dawn...

We have to reinvent our vowed
paradise,
To recreate the Eden's garden
in the rough,
To climb the luring wisdom tree,
To grab the snake and candidly
apologize...
Then ask the Lord to beg a pardon
For punishing the innocence of love,
For kicking humans from their glee...

I Stirred the Sediments

I stirred the sediments
In every bottle of my days;
After the rising sticky fear
Erased some sentiments
And wrinkles on my face;
It seems angelically clear.

The colorless moonlight
Runs like a horror movie:
The shadows kill the light,
The future is quite groovy.

My gruesome yoke of fate
Acts like a brute gendarme;
I loathe its outrageous trait,
I'll be fighting tooth and nail
Its twisted, cunning charm,
Its criminality that is on bail.

The path to bliss is paved,
The baby steps are taken,
A boisterous crowd raved,
Eternity was in the making.

I kissed goodbye the night,
I sent farewell into a day,
My ecstasy is on the way,
Long live the luring light.

Imaginary wins

"Demands of our thankfulness
Are worse than thanklessness."

This great idea caught me by surprise
And vanished on a never dusted page
As if the sun on a whim refused to rise,
And even a dawn won't leave its cage.

In spite of our David's stars or crosses,
We have in our hearts some quarters
To place those noisy slot-machines
And suffer devastating losses
After a few imaginary wins.

I am devoured by the gambling flame
That even burns my fated daily bread;
I am a needle; greed is a thread,
I move ahead and take the blame.

Incoherent

There can be only one best,
Just take my word and bank it.
The second side of any blanket
Embracing only those who rest.

The phones will ring
If there is nothing more to lose
Or when there are no more gains;
My freedom is an early spring,
It is a trusted and devoted muse,
A life without censorship or chains.

It is a lifelong flight into the space,
Away from a constant vicious race,
And from the baffling Gordian knots,
Away from a pile of incoherent dots,
Into eternity of the dreamland's light.

Inferno

My mind is still alive,
My body dwells in hell,
My soul tries to survive
Below the church's bell.

I am hardly breathing in inferno,
I am so-called al dente cooked;
My angel joyfully said buonjiorno
While flew above; he overlooked.

Instagram

My eager critics throw mud
Into the guiltless heart
Of my imagination;
It thins my blood in veins
Yet, disillusionment remains
Enfolded in frustration.

I morph my patience
Into eternity of oceans:
My being can't accept
The torrent of emotions
Devouring an ancient dam,
Destroyed by a generation
Of green avocado spreads
Convulsing on the threads,
Manipulated by Instagram…

Intriguing Scent

My angels sent her to my gloomy street,
I knew, I'll surrender if we will ever meet.
My intuition seldom fails:
Only the strings of rain
Paid tribute to the rails
Devoured by my train.

Under a swirling gold,
Playing its title role
Along the cavalcade
Of almost naked trees,
I try to cure my cold
And yet, I beg my soul,
"Please, do not fade,
I'd hate to rest in peace."

Today, a mirror on the wall
Reflects her gorgeous face;
The leaves continually fall
Into the shaky spider's lace.

In a quite lovely cul de sac,
Her flat was elegantly neat,
I tossed my jacket on the rack,
Her dress fell to my feet;
Excited bride and groom
Rapidly slid into a gawky kiss,
Into the most intriguing scent
Of innocence in bloom.

Someone invited us to bliss;
We thankfully went.

Linguistic Pulp

It's rather a bad time
To sip my coffee cup
And start another day;
My stanza is a silent mime,
It's just a linguistic futile pulp
It's hogwash on a silver tray.

And yet, another day, another love affair:
We go into my comfortable pied-a-terre,
She is a gorgeous lady of old pedigree;
Despite an elevated risk of birth defects,
She desperately craves a child from me;
She drops her skirt and personal effects;
No kisses, no foreplay; only a naked lust.

Sex is forever a fervent out-and-out must.

Manikin

The modern mindless manikins
Still try to understand and imitate
The bashful medieval harlequins,
Ignoring own predicted fate;
A comedy becomes a tragedy,
Reality turns into a foggy parody
Or rather a meek caricature,
Lackluster, pale, and immature.

I am aware of my sclerosis
And of my drug-induced psychosis;
But as a generous and loyal friend,
I am as always in high demand,
But never answer when they call,
I am not in touch with anyone at all.

I am a poked balloon that lost its air,
I am a mindless manikin,
I am a lifeless harlequin,
I wear a jacket with a pocket square.

Matrilineage

I knew quite well her mother,
We were close friends
Besides the odds and ends…

We fell in love,
Composed as hand and glove;
She was the younger image
Of the purest beauty,
A gorgeous matrilineage…

I'm sure, the devil was off duty.

Mediocre

One artist sees a yolk,
But paints the vivid sun;
The other sees the sun,
But paints a gloomy yolk…

Imagination is the future of the world,
Delusion is a creator of tomorrows;
Nobody ever heard the primal word;
And yet, the greatest talents steal;
A mediocracy just imitates or borrows.

My planet Earth still orbits like a wheel.

Messenger

Forgiven memories of souls
Fly high above the lavish yields,
Another brassy autumn strolls
Across anticipating juicy fields.

I am a friendless passenger
Riding a noisy train named life,
I am just a quiet messenger
Escaping from a futile strife.

My head-over-heels angels
Glided above and bade goodbye.
Life of religions never changes;
I thought enough to know why:
Reality is a pas de deux;
It is a unity of good and evil…
It's more than devotees can chew
In their daily life or in a retrieval
Or in a quest for the inevitable end
Of their intoxicating useless fights
Where every foe is a dear friend
Tip-toeing to the gloomy lights…

St. Peter placed me in his folder;
He liked a parrot on my shoulder.

Mine Canary

Don't ever hold your breath,
Don't be too careful, my friend;
Your so-called happy life will end
Without either tears or laughter,

Imagine nothing but your death
Forever after.

Don't ever ask a god for a refill,
Just play the given to you hand
Or simply take until the very end
Your daily bread as a bitter pill...

A day ahead of my obituary
I had a puzzling date
With my own death...
She smirked: you came too late;
Even at birth, I never had a life,
I never had a single breath...
And yet, I always thrive,
I am a living mine canary.

Misery of Wit

My youth has gone:
Our preacher told my Mom,
"Your son won't finish well,
He has no fear,
He doesn't want to hear
Our church's bell."

A noisy river of my days
Rocked sunny beaches in its shallow waters,
My night was wrapped in a worn out quilt
Of doubts, dreams, and unforgiven guilt.

War came and went just like a thunder,
I handled my distress anticipating advent,
And often saw under a mask of fancy dress
A never-ending dirty pit; it was a misery of wit.

It is too easy to get dirty,
It is so hard to wash it off,
Even when I've been very thirsty,
I couldn't drink with cattle from a trough.

I joined the strife of our progressive forces
To free ourselves from public intercourses.

Spring slowly pulls
The draperies aside;
When reason rules
The sun arrives inside.

Monolith

If there is myth,
There is a religion;
I wonder, is life a marble monolith,
Or just a fragile terracotta pigeon?

Life is a nothing burger,
Or just a solid paradigm;
Life is a firm world order,
Life is an unending crime.

Life is a greedy hoarder
Of our squandered time.

My Critics' Guillotine

My ancient table lamp was lit,
I wrote a verse and marveled,
Then rearranged it bit by bit;
The road well-traveled.

Right at the end of my nightshift.
I ask my muse, "What I possess?'
"Neither a big talent, nor a tiny gift,"
That's what she always says.

A cozy comfort of my morning,
It is not dull and never boring,
It is my daily fruitful routine,
Beyond my critics' guillotine.

They see no forest
For the trees,
They see no florist
For the bees.

These oracles of knowledge
Didn't descend from bliss,
These troubadours of carnage
Ascend from the abyss,
And put a stick into my spokes,
For them I am just a hoax.

I am like an actor in silent films:
I cry, nobody hears,
I talk, nobody listens.
Sometimes I change my gears,
But I am still the same,
No money and no fame.

Mysterious

It is extremely strange of being old:
A planet Earth is not my household:

What I foresaw, you'll be seeing,
But I will never see;
My views are coming into being,
While I'm still in the pursuit of glee...

At times, I am powerless,
I can no longer
Tolerate my pains;
I cry, I curse and scream...
Until it's over or unless
My will to live turns stronger
Than iffy doubts in my veins.

Bliss waits above the Earth,
Mysterious as childbirth.

Nocturnal

It's hard to hop on feet of clay,
It's hard to fly above the fray:
I hear the loud heartfelt sighs,
I pour dead-ends of our lives
In each of offered to me glass;
Red velvet of a luscious wine
Reflects a nightly silver grass
Fully belonging to moonshine;
I think I am unjustly left alone
To hold a bag of daily sorrows;
I am sure I must create a clone
That grasps but never borrows.

I jumped through many hoops,
I crossed too many futile lines,
I entertained myself with "oops"
While gliding through stop signs.
.

My scientific efforts are in vain,
My gluttony is an everlasting joy,
Unstoppable as a chronic pain,
And all-inclusive as the evil ploy.

I reach the skies, the heaven cries;
I'd rather bend and touch the land.
The oldest paradigm is broken;
"You're a winner", God has spoken.

Omar Khayyam

One has to think, create or doubt;
Dementia won't ever come about;
Please, be advised:
A brain is just a muscle exercised;
Fruitful lives are roads of the wise.

Try to be happy at the moment,
This moment is your life;
Try to be kind to your opponent,
And he will toss away his knife.

Wine grabs my hand
And ushers to a hidden part of me;
Without drinking, I would never land
On grass with morning dew of glee.

One shouldn't worry for the world,
One probably is weak and small;
Please, take my heartfelt word:
Learn all the best; not best of all.

If you don't want tomorrows,
Imagine something very bright,
Then watch your daily sorrows,
They will abandon your insight.

A road to hell is paved and wide,
I cast the dice and place my bet.
What keeps me from a suicide?
A sense of humor and my debt.

Ovations

The Holy Trinity
Plus good and evil
Equals five;
I wonder who of them
Already sent a bullet
That snatched my life.

We hardly ever die
From old and nasty age;
We die from our wounds;
We turn the final page
And humbly bid goodbye.

Art is a talking to the dead,
Just heartfelt conversations;
I am sure; I am not too bad,
My verses often earn ovations.

Parables

I live the days long passed;
I am a little extra in this film,
New tunes are hard-and-fast,
I am not a famous movie star;
I am lackluster, I don't gleam;
I am just a badly tuned guitar.

For me
Reality is a pictorial space
Filled with the futile parables
About our bewildered glee
Without any integrity and grace;
Both died with a heroic Heracles.

Only in the fairytales
We are so tightly bound
To pay for our bad affairs
The second time around:
My buddies went to heaven,
While I am still on cloud nine;
I am committing all the seven,
Yet, I am sailing in a luscious wine.

Perception

I am stuck in my linguistic whining,
And possibly won't rest on laurels,
Or wrapped in the Turin shroud;
I missed the Declaration signing,
I only saw a silver lining of a cloud
That flew above my tainted morals.

The verse isn't a spectator's couch,
It is, at times, a cruel contact sport;
And while the poets murmur ouch,
The critics disrespectfully snort.

The eye of the beholder
Is only the evenhanded referee
Within the everlasting conflict
Between depiction and perception
I see a tiny glimpse of glee…

Pianos

I drink my whiskey from a firehose,
I even learned to square the circles,
I often balance pianos on my nose;
In politics I shun the reds and blues,
I close my eyes and vote for purples,
I'd like to hear their scheming news.

A life ends only once
In a blue moon,
And when death comes,
We sing the same old tune
"Amazing Grace"…

In any case,
Life surely takes its toll.

I've been betrayed
By my resilience;
I cast no shadows on the wall
As if I'm a saint forever sinless.

Although, I don't believe in bliss,
I don't believe in the abyss;
That's why death didn't grant me
Her final life freezing kiss of glee.

Plainly

I am the one, who plainly loves,
Who can effectively encourage
To lock our frustrations' storage
With iron hands in velvet gloves.

A waterfall of swirling snowflakes
Like twinkling shawls or garlands,
Mildly descends and calmly lands
On our cold and shaky shoulders;
Even a winter knows what it takes
To thrill the eyes of the beholders.

I knelt:
Become my wife,
I'll love you all my life,
I'll be a wind just to caress you,
I'll be a shadow just to follow you,
I'll be the sun to warmly love you.

To no avail; the snow didn't melt.

Political Note

There is nothing left
For my imagination;
My reckless nation
Performed a bare striptease;
Even the sunlit clouds wept
With the intolerable freeze.

Premonition

Life is a war; I went to fight…

Please, wait; I will return;
Trust me; there will be light,
Just wait, no matter what,
Just wait, as long it may take;
Wars never gift us a shortcut,
But once in a blue moon a break.

Just wait and I will earn
Your patience and your love,
On Earth and far above,
On Earth and even after…

In premonition of the promised bliss,
In premonition of the eternal kiss;
In premonition of the eternal laughter,
In premonition of the infinite disaster.

War doesn't hold its breath:
I whisper my so long, farewell, adieu;
I am too far away from you,
But only a few steps from death.

Prose

Beers, wines?
I am not exactly sure;
But when it is a little late,
Cognac, tequila, vodka
I am familiar with my fate;
I am a poetic lunch du jour.

I am both transparent and opaque,
It's what my parents tried to make;
They've never fallen into a gloom,
They liked to see my talents bloom.

They recognized my urge to be myself
And carve my verses; not a lazy prose
To gather dust on a well-forgotten shelf,
While I am waiting on my wobbling toes.

Some put a ton of raisins
In a small loaf of bread,
But it is still a loaf of bread
And not a mountain of raisins.

Quality

I am a fortune cookie writer,
I am a truth-foreseeing fighter,
I work as know-it-all predictor;
I morph a loser into a victor.

From start to finish and beyond
Life is a painful engagement:
Instead of pen-and-ink my verses
And getting results I never meant;
I use only my jewels and morsels
And wait for my critics to respond.

In our existence I miss a quality
That not anymore occurs in life:
I wore a smart mask, not a witty,
I chose a striking lover not a wife.

Regrettably

In the pursuit of truly happy times,
I plucked a good-luck-five-petals clover;
I search for punishments without crimes;
Regrettably, my fruitful pursuits are over.

A tender dawn and a fiery sunrise
Wrapped tunes of happiness and sent
To our bleeding hearts and loud cries;
Regrettably, it only hit the vent…

Nobody reads the ancient comedies,
We keep them on a dusty shelf,
They turn into the modern tragedies;
Regrettably, our history repeats itself.

A blade-thin beam of a red-hot light
Streams on my squeaky parquet floor
As a forewarning of a bloody fight;
Regrettably, another fool declared a war.

Reins

We fear our faithful Apocalypse,
Our deadly inescapable eclipse.

I scooped this awful fairytale
From my God-fearing breath:
The white and red,
The black and pale;
Conquest and war,
Famine and death.

These artfully hued
Foretellers of our Lord's arrival,
These four apocalyptic horses
Remind me of my feisty verses:
I'm talented enough to be a rival
In this gods-versus-humans feud,
To practice my idealistic quatrains,
To wrench those ugly horses' reins.

Restful

The merciless claws of life
Don't scratch me anymore,
Don't leave the ugly scars:
From eight to five
I am working like a whore
Then I am drinking in the bars.

I am not coldblooded and neither pokerfaced:
You easily may feel my strong emotions,
Or possibly the memory of them...
My wrinkles never knew the modern lotions,
I lived the way I have been raised
From exodus toward the star of Bethlehem.

Perhaps in vain, I try to bring a subtle harmony
To our apprehensive and often broken hearts...
At times, a veiled, old-fashioned sweetness
Of my sardonic, spicy irony
Spun thirsty unexciting souls toward the arts
And gives our bodies some completeness.

I watch the strings of beams,
The rainy clouds flank the sky;
My restless past still dreams,
My restful future sadly cries.

Retreat

Life talked to me a lot:
Each t was crossed,
Each i received a dot,
Each dice was tossed.

My mind has been a hot retreat
For rather not deliberate desires.
I never took a comfortable seat
To watch the sunsets' fires...

As always, head over heels,
I nurtured my demanding life
With lavishly exquisite meals,
Great wines and loyal friends;
And often catch a flying knife
Sent by my dearest fiends...

My mind is still a calm retreat
For my unintentional desires.

Sappy

The angels watched from the above,
I touched a coffin resting on the table,
And sent farewell to one I used to love
For many, many troubled years,
Although, it sounds like a sappy fable,
I couldn't stop the river of my tears...

I'm sure; lives don't disappear in death,
I hear a new one in a baby's breath.

Scherzo

Life is still banging on my door,
But lags behind the rite of spring.
I peeled my shadow off the floor
And soared into the blue to sing.

I passed the devil on the left,
God passed me on the right,
I was quite young and deft,
No one could stop my flight.

Although, Good Friday passed,
Jesus has died then resurrected
To care for chosen and selected;
Regrettably, this vow didn't last.

But then,
The wicked evidence was raked
As a strong rejection of the past,
Even
Orgasms of history were faked!

Bright Easter and Passover gone,
Lackluster days are here to stay,
Only the sparrows chirp at dawn
Expecting yet another sunny day.

Scrambled

I'm right in the middle of a scrambled wasteland,
Lavishly fertilized by our skepticism and doubts,
Under the instinctive yet still impending nihilism;
I hear the tunes of loud sugarcoated optimism
Delivered by the creepy Dixie marching band
Escorting a pine top casket
With a chain sawed crucifix;
Just like a pique-nique basket
With my delusional idee fixe…

That truth at afternoon,
Is still the truth at night;
I hope to see you soon;
Let there be light!

She Was a Perfect Trooper

Among the nightly wizards,
She was a gutsy alligator,
Among the lounge lizards
She was the fastest waiter,
Even in a drunken stupor
She was a perfect trooper.

She cursed between her laughs,
I liked it very much, it was iconic;
Her life-size naked photographs
Where seductively quadrophonic;
She barked her filthy paragraphs,
As always tongue-in-cheek; ironic.

I tossed the dice
And won the prize,
I held her in my arms,
Devouring her charms.

I am a hunter, I eat my kill,
I am a man, I need a thrill,
If it's a lady hard-to-get; I'll wait;
But most of us will bite the bait.

In any case, I tossed the dice,
It landed well, I won the prize,
And held her in my arms,
Devouring her tasty charms.

Silence of Pain or Pain of Silence

There are too many things
That can't be seen or heard:
A melancholy on a menu a la cart,
Silence of pain or pain of silence,
The silence of a broken heart,
The pain of an irrational defiance,
The silence of a violin without strings,
The pain of a wingless firebird,
Unanswered loves that died in vain,
Or just the morals' tarnished pain...

Our days are breeding grounds,
Under the looming clouds,
No matter shine or rain.
Why can't we bear the pain?
Our time has almost passed,
Time couldn't melt the ice,
We veered from blast to blast,
Collecting pains for our paradise.

There are no metronomes of time,
The silent pains don't cry or sing,
They carry their predestined cross;
Only the actions of a silent mime
Remind us of a fearless albatross
Concealing pains of a broken wing.

The dogs and seagulls face the wind,
The humans turn their backs and pray,
The birds and dogs have never sinned,
Or maybe angels looked the other way.

We can't survive without sins
The truce is generally holding
Between the friends and fiends;
Triumphant banners are unfolding
Behind the runners from the winds.

Singer

I knew you've heard
I am a decent singer,
Almost a mockingbird;
You're my lady friend,
I never had a finger
For a wedding bend…

Slide out of your dress
Unfurl your golden hair,
I'm so eager to caress
The wreck of our affair.

I raked some tiny beads
Of my devoured youth;
The past repeats to hurt;
Never to soothe…

Slept

If death ever slept
We could arrive to our dreams,
The boneyards would remain unkept.

No mourns, no woes or so it seems.

We don't forget the dead
Only the livings are forgotten;
We get the promised daily bread,
But only chew the fat and cotton.

The gluttony is thrilling,
Life-dealer runs the table;
Who disagrees or fights against?
No one is willing;
No one is able.
Our greed is too intense.

I wrote my parting book;
My time is paralyzed...
The critics bit the final hook,
My soul is paradised.

Soar

I write; my anguish surges
Into collided flashy rhymes;
Meanwhile, my irritated wisdom urges
To bring some priceless silent mimes.

And yet, my awkward mind is a retreat
For most of my obscure desires;
It's a back alley; it's a hopeless street,
It's a flea market with no buyers.

Rene Descartes once said,
I think, therefore I am alive;
I can't repeat this anymore.
I lost my lifelong literary strife,
Only the bitter memories still soar...

Solitude

Solitude was a disaster in my youth,
But such a pleasure in maturity;
Today, even the smallest bits of truth
Caress my innocence and purity.

Not everything will end
With my inevitable death;
I will survive in hearts
Of foes and friends
I left behind;
They will preserve the truth,
They heard my parting breath.

Squared

I quickly redefined the troubles
Intensely worrying my mind;
There is no virtue in the bubbles;
I resurrected my ancestral bind.

God charges me for daily bread,
Although, I used to get it free.
Please wait; I'm not yet dead;
I firmly stand; I'm not a fallen tree.

My circles are forever squared;
A hoary task impossible no more,
The shocking news was shared,
The loud echoes will forever roar.

The mindless manikins have realized
That good is evil but artfully disguised

Stage

We never meet our saints,
At times, we recognize a sin;
While red blood runs in our veins
Into a heart whether you lose or win.

We're not exactly proud of the past:
Some of the wins were rather sordid;
The generals were lavishly awarded
In spite of a sullen, gloomy overcast.

They placed us on the stage
And flaunted as the valued arts;
Then locked that golden cage
When saw a void in our hearts.

The shiny uniforms of heroes
Send our egos to the stars,
And only the dusty mirrors
Show our wounds and scars.

Stance

Split-tailed martins are flying low,
The storm is looming awfully high,
The merciless winds already blow
Between my castles in the sky.

The filthiest dump trucks
Perform their fumy work rendition;
Lined like the ducks,
Like ballerinas for a new audition.

It is a time of dancing bears,
Of carnivals and fire-eaters,
Of acrobats on the trapeze;
It is a time of topless girls
Chasing in fast two-seaters
The men who nearly rest in peace.

A time when space and distance
Have hardly any meaning:
There is no age and no mortality;
Only the guilty conscience reeling
In this confused and cloudy reality
Of our ground-breaking stance.

Stars fade then die

The stars don't outlive
The sinners anymore,
We are exactly even;
They faint and leave,
No hope for an encore;
Forgotten and forgiven.

Stars fade then die,
And shyly disappear
Into the endless sky;
I want my angel sing
First far then near,
While our bells still ring

I see their flying souls,
Good things end well,
Stars left black holes
And roared farewell,
It was the primal word
That started our world.

Still soar

What's going on above?
The same what is below;
I wonder if there is a love,
That lets our passions glow.

I borrow wisdom from my doubts,
I am never blindly introverted;
I am a banner for the timid crowds,
I am a window into a life converted.

My intellect distills
A waterfall of useless bouts
That used to turn the wheels
Of my soul's pains and shouts.

Nobody cares about what I knew
Unless they know that I care
About the chosen few;
About those who fought in war
During the endless days and nights;
My agonizing memories still soar
Toward the new war's horrid sights.

Tags

We the unwilling
Led by the unqualified
Into the art of killing,
While our mothers cried,
Receiving the neatly folded flags
And bags or coffins with the tags...

The City Chaos is in Order

Life-juror disregards my valor,
A verdict is in black and white,
A rainbow lost its yellow color,
A raven-cloud blocks the light.

I play my old accordion; you like my stuff,
The show goes on, it is my one-way love.

The city chaos is in order, even the disarray of Broadway;
I gather thoughts and solder a bridge into the Milky Way.

We drift apart; I am on the way to fix for us some drinks;
Your iceberg-heart will melt one day while wisdom blinks.

The scent of pumpkin bread,
The sound of a falling apple,
Those days are quickly fled,
Only the bloody sabers rattle;
I dust my moth-eaten uniform
To fight another futile storm.

My merciless death was never crowned,
I held my final breath, I was love-bound.

I will be back; war isn't the end of lives,
I will be back, if our tired love survives,
I will be back before our stars are fallen,
I will be back before your heart is stolen,
I will be back, only the dead have seen the end.

The Crescent Learns to Fly

My angel hovers in the sky,
The stars shine on his face;
The crescent learns to fly
Before the sun's embrace.

We tango to the end of night,
I kiss blue sadness of her eyes;
Hopes drown in the melting ice,
Love has no future in plain sight.

We graduated from the night;
New dawn erases our tears,
Our love fades into the light,
Into the heartless crowd's jeers.

And only my subconscious
Whispers, "spring is upon us:
The seeds of cherries
Are waiting in the frozen ground,
And very soon, the berry-fairies
Will show off their taste around."

The Enigmatic Doorway

The future is devouring itself,
The wars kidnapped our lives,
Even a hallow portrait of myself
Was varnished with my lies.

The enigmatic doorway
Hid images of badness;
A trembling candle on the tray
Became a sunlit night of sadness.

My books snooze on the shelves,
They are the tragedies of love:
Banalities unleashed themselves,
But didn't bring us close enough.

I never learned to fly and crawl
Under the arches of rainbows;
I barely know anything at all
Beyond my foes stone's throws.

The muddy river of my verses
Runs towards poetic carnage,
Towards my critics' daily curses,
Under the futile tree of knowledge.

The Eve of a New Year

Some crawl, the others fly;
Life-teacher is quite stern,
I study our history to learn
How to eat and have the pie.

Our gods forever say,
They like the thrifty,
Those who just take
But never give away.
Only the fallen angel
Unwillingly stays guilty.

Confessions fell into the dust
Like teardrops of strong men,
Who earned their angel's trust;
He left; they didn't notice when.

Euphoria and trepidation:
The eve of a New Year,
Farewell to what was dear,
I am in the midst of cheers,
But try to leave this jubilation
To close my eyes,
To calm my sighs,
And hide my tears.

The Fallen Rise

The tender hearts of friends,
The glossy wedding bands,
Retain the memories of me,
I pay the price for being free,
The past is definitely closed,
I wander as a drifting ghost.

I mask and veil my face,
I am a scout in disguise,
I walk across the maze,
I see the fallen try to rise.

Beasts run the fields,
Birds pierce the air;
The future always yields
Only for those who dare.

Old branches lash the clouds,
White cotton hid away the sky,
The tiny twigs as lacy shrouds
Cover all those who cannot fly.

The Primary Colors

Under a blue ocean of the sky,
Over the sandy yellow spread,
When our foes or brothers die
Their bloods look similarly red.

We went to war. We went to hell.
Our happy futures promptly died,
We couldn't hear the church's bell,
But heard when our mothers cried.

The drums of war were awfully loud,
The artist-war tinted the heavens red,
But a pure kindness of a leaded cloud
Descended like a shroud on the dead.

War-mongers need their dire treats,
Therefore, the horrid history repeats:
The stars and crosses of the fallen,
Remind of our lives timelessly stolen.

In wars we make our kills,
Push consciousness aside,
But at the end, nobody wins,
War is a bloody game of suicide.

Their Wreaths Fell Down

Dunes whisper to the wind,
The ebbs caress the sand,
And tease the fishing gear;
A sign "Keep off" is pinned,
Abandoned and unmanned
Slanting the trembling pier.

The sailors went to fish,
Their wives must wait,
Sharing a single wish:
Return, despite the fate.

The boat was beaten by the storm,
Only the hungry seagulls swarm
Above the drowned sailors.
The saints, the fishermen of souls,
Will hide their sins and failures
From the tattered Dead Sea Scrolls.

Poor wives may hope and wait,
But dreams will let them drown;
They will follow the old-style trait,
And climb that trembling pier,
And let their wreaths fall down.

Tightly locked

I was invited by my critics to a dinner:
I've read and later served my verses;
To make me feel like a worthy winner,
They keenly wolfed them at the tables
Then clapped with hooves like horses
That chewed their straw in the stables.

At last, I pulled a rabbit from a hat:
I sang; the audience was shocked;
As if I hit them with a baseball bat;
I knew, I reached the door of fame,
Unfortunately, the door was locked.

The snobbish strangers were appalled
By my, as they insisted, awkward style,
Although, my poems positively trolled;
I was quite sharp; I didn't chew the fat.
These days, with laughs or just a smile
On my beer budget I often drink "Moet".

I stood before the door and knocked.
The door of fame was tightly locked.

Tomorrows

Tomorrows of my past
Are unpredictable, at times;
I often try to change my mind,
Since I am a lifetime sinking boat
Without sails and with a broken mast.
Nevertheless, my lines still smoothly float,
And I am old, but my obituary is not yet signed.

After I lost confusions of my generation,
I looked for truth and climbed the tallest hill;
The tunes of passions, loves and tears
Quietly fall on my idle-half-deaf ears,
But sadly fail to keep me on my toes…
My heartfelt poetry becomes a prose.
So far, I found just a single God's creation:
My death and tears of those who'll pay the bill.

Tooth and Nail

A poet wannabe,
A movie star who didn't make it,
A humble girl who whispers yes,
But never no or maybe,
The worshipers without any faith
But learned to fake it...

I say hello and shake their hands,
But truly wonder: foes or friends?

I am always fighting tooth and nail,
To catch a wind by my poetic sail...

Tour de Force

Art is a lie creating truth,
Art is a magic saving youth,
Art is a requiem
For souls that locked in cages,
For poetry of yet unwritten pages,
For our sins unknown to remorse.

Art is a requiem
For the integrity in our lives,
For our futile but merciless strifes.

Art is a requiem for those
Who've seen the end of peace,
Who fought the brutal evil force,
Encircled by the burning trees...
Art is a requiem for those
Who've seen the end of wars.

Art is my Pegasus,
My muse, my loyal winged horse;
Art is the only known tour de force.

Twigs

The moon is glowing,
It knows our intrigues,
The wind is blowing.
Young lilacs' twigs
Whip dusty windows
Of our country digs.

I am revisiting my past,
My wars with wives and lovers,
I am a drifting boat; no mast,
Only the albatross still hovers.

Someone may take,
Someone may give,
I entertain them with a fake
That I forget whom I forgive.

I choked my wicked youth
In favor of intense athletics,
In vain, I tried to soothe
The wounds of my genetics.

I missed my lucky train,
I learned to bear my pain,
My eyes are always dry,
I didn't want to learn to cry.

Two Silky Threads

The rails look like two silky threads
Intriguing, shiny, long and straight;
I hope this railroad never ends,
My memories are hidden in its freight.

It is my remaining life, it is my title role
It is the closing road of my quest;
I took the worst, I took the best,
I took a bag with marvels of my soul.

My daring life is like a terrifying film
That runs the past before my eyes:
Some happy years, some very grim,
Some victories, some truths and lies.

I grieve my buddies, they were the best,
A blanket of the night fell on their chests,
I clinch my teeth; my eyes refuse to cry.
I used to know every soul that went to fly.

It doesn't come as a surprise,
The sun will also rise.

Uniform

A lull before the storm...
A single battle left,
Just one more sin;
I pulled my uniform,
It will be hard to win,
I am no longer deft.

There is no love that lasts,
We learned the truth today:
We failed to fuse our pasts;
We failed to see another way.

Although, love isn't wise,
It turns the world,
It runs our lives,
It is a mighty sword.

Old night is dark,
Dawn yet is frail;
There is no happy lark,
There is no singing nightingale.

It is a lull before the storm,
I went to pawn my uniform.

Vacant Inns

My church won't usher me to bliss,
It simply scares me with the abyss.

My logics crumble at the seams
When I recall Ignatius Loyola:
The ends won't justify the means
Whether I play a flute or a viola.

Noon is a time to ring the bell,
Is it a time to get the wind
And be forever free?
Is it a time to pull my soul and sell
Before I sinned,
Or humbly ask, to be or not to be?

The boneyards have some vacant inns;
The polished tombstones hide our sins.

Vertebrate

I am a vertebrate:
I hardly ever crawl,
I am a little humped but straight;
I never weasel; I am not a snake,
I'd rather run or stroll;
I fall, stand up, and never break.

I take my creativity
Over banality and certainty;
I take my innocent naivety
Over a doted i or a crossed t.

Over the common always,
Over the stubborn never,
I'd rather drink the brine
Of loneliness and sorrows:
The nectar of the gods,
The holy grail of wine,
The great pinot noir,
The never-failing star
Against the tricky odds

Waiting

This world of violence
Is not a space to meet our gods,
It's not a valid place in any sense,
No one enjoys the lightning rods.

A loud, tone-deaf marching band
Is a well-tolerated cultural ambush;
I am familiar with my empty hand;
I cannot guess what's in the bush.

They used to be birds of a feather,
These days, they're the birds of prey;
When they start circling in the sky,
I'll write my will and say goodbye.

I didn't buy a modern dictionary;
With Google no one learns to spell;
Although, I'm drinking from that well,
And slowly writing my own obituary.

The bitter end is trying to break in,
Meanwhile, my passing is delayed;
The benches in the sun are taken,
I am humbly waiting in the shade.

Wall

In any case, I've been unusually paid
For helping those who were betrayed;
My certitude and kindness were ridiculed,
I was called arrogant and even schooled.

I need to have a little bit of grit,
I drown like a hopeless louche, .
I've reached my end of wit
And act like a bad-tempered grouch.
My ex flaunts newest fashions on runways,
While I am still sleeping on a scruffy couch
With masochistic pleasures of dismays…

I lived through happy days,
I tasted some bitter fruits of life,
I strolled between my gains and losses,
My truck devoured dozens of highways
As if I tried to catch a quickly falling knife
And hit my grave under the quiet crosses.

I've seen and done it all,
I've been a coward and a hero;
Any experience is just a rearview mirror,
But I had learned to wait…
I am still looking for a sacred hidden gate
To a promised bliss beyond the solid wall.

We walk

We walk,
We pass habitual bookinists…
The flows of the river Seine…
Worn manuscripts in tatters...

We walk,
We make our fits and twists,
Mourn losses, longing gains,
Seeing the liabilities of men,
Revisit the exalting matters,
Dismiss exaggerated pains.

We talk,
Each word evokes
A brushstroke of a painting;
My rhymes induce
A state of wonder,
The imagery lingers in the sky,
Your lovely head
Is resting on my shoulder,
The mystery of glee is fainting,
But wouldn't say goodbye…

Whatsoever

I walk the jungle of your book,
Along the verses snugly twined;
I am still hanging on the hook,
As sharp as your sarcastic mind.

The ice wrapped our love's creek,
Protecting its impervious mystique,
That looks like a neglected shrine
Or rather too-late warning sign…

Your thoughts in every phrase
Reminds me of the finest lace
Of whole-hearted words of praise
Caressing your still gorgeous face.

The oneness of our chill and fever
Demolished by a merciless cleaver
Forever; not for never
And no one noticed whatsoever.

Why

I dash across the sunlit night
A falcon cuts the sunlight flow,
Why do we always fight?
Why can't we let it go?
Why do we build a wall?
Why don't we enjoy the sight?
There's enough of light for all
Under the arches of rainbow.

Why do we try to break or bend?
Why can't we try to fix or mend?

Whether we are indicted or incited,
Both chairs reserved for the invited,
Both roads veer like the thrown dice
To gates of the abyss and paradise.

Don't wake me up,
Don't mess with my nightmares,
Don't spill illusions from my cup,
Let me ascend the promised stairs.

Wolfing

I like my constant stress,
My issues don't require
Immediate solutions…
If God is willing,
I'll forget the dead
But mourn the living
And their contributions
In wolfing our daily bread.

I traced the genesis:
Absence of evidence
Steered us into religions
And we remain blind pigeons
That shot the piano player,
But blamed the Matthew prayer.

Working Girl

I guess, it was the time for me to fail,
I searched for peace in a safe haven,
I combed through every little street,
Unfortunately, in vain, to no avail,
I looked for a saint, but I met a raven,
And wondered who arranged this treat.

I meandered down here-she flew,
We looked into each other's eyes,
No feathers roughed, no injured pride,
We knew, we both were in disguise,
We were interrelated; here is a clue:
Her skin is black, but I am black inside.

I wrote as every poet, my sermon on the mount
As the whole-hearted songs;
It was a perfect moment to keep a sharp account
Of what were rights or wrongs.

I wrote it for this charming raven, a pretty but ill-mannered girl,
This Orleans' scorched maiden, mysterious in her majestic role,
I trembled, I was eager to unfurl
The banner of her heart and soul.

She was a working girl; she gave me what I asked;
She was a precious pearl, magnificent but masked.
As in the story of Magdalene, nobody dared to cast a stone,
She was so innocently clean; the gods and saints still moan.

Worries

It takes immense creative struggle;
It takes a long exiting journey
Toward a convoluted jungle
Of modern unforgiving art,
So vast, Intolerant and thorny;

Toward a pure nonfigurative art;
Without sad or happy stories,
Without passions, calm or worries.

Critics are mocking,
God didn't save,
My art is rocking
On a stormy wave.

It does quite well,
Perhaps in vain;
The time will tell
To pack for bliss or hell.

Wreath

My premonition seldom fails,
Days run like the strings of rain,
As quickly as the polished rails,
Devoured by my lifelong train.

I couldn't find peace on pages
Of a leather-bound Book of Life;
I failed to soothe my daily rages
With yet another gorgeous wife...

Sugar gets on my nerves
And daily hurts my teeth;
I outlived another vicious foe,
Life is arranged as quid-pro-quo:
I guess, not every grave deserves
A marble tombstone and a wreath.

A naughty morning breeze
Disturbs the scent of lavender,
And whispers to the golden trees,
Your time has come, surrender,
If this is not your paradise, what is?

Youth

Where is my youth along a fertile pasture?
Where is that blissful and dreamy place?
Where is the bird of hope I tried to capture?
Where is the garden of my innocence?

Where are the days of common sense?
Where are the guards of youth and friends?
Where are the roses, where are the thorns?
Where are the kings to occupy the thrones?

Where is the splendor a gliding swan?
Where is my granny's lily pond?
Where is the blinding, smiling sun?
Where is the monolith of our bond?

First date, first kiss, the first love ever,
I left behind those faded days forever,
I left the slimy moat of tears and pains,
I left the quagmires of greed and gains.

The malachite of grass is luminous but coy,
A nervous butterfly swirls like an autumn leaf,
Her wings are trembling with impatient joy,
Her happiness is timeless, her agony is brief.

I miss the doubts of my grief-stricken soul,
The stronghold of my curiosity was blown,
I walk the enigmatic path towards my goal,
I walk across my past into a life well-known.

Retreat

Life talked to me a lot:
Each t was crossed,
Each i received a dot,
Each dice was tossed.

My mind has been a hot retreat
For rather not deliberate desires.
I never took a comfortable seat
To watch the sunsets' fires…

As always, head over heels,
I nurtured my demanding life
With lavishly exquisite meals,
Great wines and loyal friends;
And often catch a flying knife
Sent by my sweetheart fiends…

My mind is still a calm retreat
For my unintentional desires.

Wrapped

Our history is a never-ending journey
Into the deepest cells of human souls,
Of those who lived and died before;
Nobody needs a power of attorney,
Nobody needs to climb the tallest walls
To see or learn what they were dying for.

And yet, whether or not we know history,
The past is a puzzle wrapped in mystery.

Acknowledgements

I am deeply grateful to Judith Broadbent
For her uniquely skilled guidance and generous stewardship
For her unyielding yet wise editing which gives me enough space
To freely exercise my whims.

I'd like to thank Kate Broadbent
for her exquisitely nuanced suggestions and her deep understanding of poetic imagery.

To all my friends for their genuine advice and enthusiasm.

Printed in the United States
by Baker & Taylor Publisher Services